The cover is a picture of the Gulf of Mexico
from the beach in Destin, Florida

MARINELLA F. MONK, MD

GENTLE THERAPY

*Converting daily activities
into kind, gentle, and rewarding therapy
for the mind, body, and soul.*

Inspiring Voices®
A Service of **Guideposts**

Dr. Monk also wrote 'You Are Not Alone' in 2010, and excellent
source of strength, confidence, and encouragement for each
of us as we confront the challenges and difficulties of life in
the 21st Century. 'You Are Not Alone' is available worldwide
through www.Amazon.com, and in most bookstores.

Inspiring Voices books may be ordered through
booksellers or by contacting:

Inspiring Voices
1663 Liberty Drive
Bloomington, IN 47403
www.inspiringvoices.com
1-(866) 697-5313

ISBN: 978-1-4624-0190-1 (sc)
ISBN: 978-1-4624-0191-8 (e)

Library of Congress Control Number: 2012941491

Printed in the United States of America

Inspiring Voices rev. date: 06/29/2012

I dedicate this book to my grandson, Alexandre Ioan, wishing that it will bring him inspiration and guidance as he grows to become an adult.

My gratitude goes to my family and my friends, who have been such a blessing to me. I felt privileged treating my patients who have proven to me that a positive, cheerful, and unselfish approach to life has wondrous healing effects.

My husband, Robert, will always be in my heart with love, for believing in me, offering unconditional support, and showing me how love can be the Gentlest Therapy.

"To enjoy good health, to bring true happiness to one's family, to bring peace to all, one must first discipline and control one's own mind. If a man can control his mind he can find the way to Enlightenment, and all wisdom and virtue will naturally come to him."

Buddha, founder of Buddhism, 563-483 BC

"Come to me, all you that are weary and are carrying heavy burdens, and I will give you rest, for I am gentle and humble at heart, and you will find rest for your souls."

Matthew 11-28

CHAPTERS

1. What is Gentle Therapy? 1
2. Know Yourself 7
3. Good Things Await You 15
4. Your Home, Your Sanctuary 31
5. Finding Peace and Serenity 41
6. Healing Therapy 53
7. Loving Therapy 71
8. Playtime Therapy 85
9. Pet Therapy 101
10. Finding Beauty in Art 113
11. Our Hobbies 123
12. The Universe 135
13. Connecting with the Divine 147
14. Music Therapy 157
15. Prayer Therapy 169
    Conclusion 185
    Acknowledgements 187
    Comments from readers 189

1 - WHAT IS GENTLE THERAPY?

Gentle Therapy is not a new idea, and comfort and wellbeing therapies have been offered to the public in many different ways. From the early times of human existence, many civilizations have introduced the concept of fulfilling our need for quiet moments of contemplation and meditation, in the constant quest for a better quality of life.

Ancient Egyptians were present in the Nile valley as early as 5500 BC, and they developed an advanced technology never before encountered in architectural, agricultural, or military aspects of their lives. Medicine and religion were also important parts of their civilization. They employed astonishing surgical procedures, but also strongly believed that every human being is made of physical and spiritual aspects, all intertwined, as part of a cosmic and immortal dimension. In their daily lives, ancient Egyptians placed great value on their appearance and hygiene, along with a developed taste for beauty of their clothing, jewelry and accessories, their home decoration, and their cultural activities. Music and prayer were part of regular activities, and whole arrays of instruments were played, including the harp, considered to be the oldest musical instrument.

Many other civilizations of the past show that people gave an important place to the manner in which they lived, and that being surrounded by beauty and art, and finding peace and serenity represented their main aspirations in life.

Greeks, Romans, Assyrians and Babylonians, Chinese, Persians, Minoans, Celts, Hebrews, Dacians,

1

Thracians, Mayans, Incas and Aztecs, to name only some of them, all included in their cultures the practice and search for tranquility.

Nowadays, the idea of a more gentle therapy to bring wellbeing into our lives was introduced several decades ago, and encompasses a multitude of interventions and methods of treatment offered by an even larger variety of practitioners from different backgrounds.

From holistic, craniosacral, or Thai massage and gentle touch, to ear/foot therapy, aromatherapy, rhythms Yoga, pathways colonics, or chiropractic lipossage, to name just a few, one can find a number of ways to get nonconventional interventions.

I believe that many of them are well intended and efficient, and most of the therapists are qualified and provide alternative choices in their treatments.

As a physician, I feel that our profession places us in a very special position when dealing with so many aspects of human suffering, from devastating physical limitations, to visceral and moral pain. We are trained in making the diagnostic of a variety of conditions, as we are versed in the use of advanced diagnostic technology and providing different therapies when approaching different conditions.

But, we physicians would certainly benefit from learning more about natural methods of intervention, so we can teach our patients how to use them on their own, and on a regular basis.

We are already very privileged when establishing relationships with our patients, perhaps comparable only to the one existing with our ministers. We are *privy to the patient's most intimate problems, and have the special honor of confidentiality in our relations with patients. When they grant us trust, he or she relies on our help.*

Here is when I want to offer all my energy and the knowledge I have acquired over so many years of training, in order to make sure that this person will reach the best condition possible. Besides treating my patients' medical problems, I want them to know that I profoundly care for their quality of life, and that they have a new ally in their quest to achieve a better level of physical and mental wellbeing.

Gentle is a word I like to use as meaning LOVE. My intention is to associate the meaningful aspects of our lives with the feeling of warmth, sweetness, and happiness of love. I believe that love transcends time, survives periods of violence, and represents the most significant element of the human nature.

To me, the most extraordinary example of universal love was shown to us by Jesus Christ. As a mortal being, He was subjected to trials and tribulations; as a divine presence, He responded with love to the suffering inflicted on Him. He did all this to show humanity that, in the end, nothing is more important than love. And 2000 years later, billions of people honor this message. 2000 years later, after wars and unspeakable cruelties have ravaged the ages, what has survived many events longtime forgotten, is love, as the most significant and everlasting element of the human condition.

I intend to show in this book that in order to improve our way of living and dealing with everyday's problems, one does not necessarily need to go to some place to get one hour or so of therapy and relaxation after a difficult day. My approach is to introduce Gentle Therapy as a way to improve our every day way of living, and create the habit to carry with us and employ Gentle Therapy everywhere we are and everywhere we go.

Writing the different chapters of this book, I wanted to take my reader on a voyage, linking different therapies with the sensation imprinted by diverse places, and when possible, accompanied by an extraordinary piece of music. The feeling I intended to produce can be greatly enhanced by visual associations of a unique location, while the suggested music can create a strong emotional atmosphere.

Because of my earlier exposure in life to classical music, the reader will forgive me if the music I refer to will be classical, but I promise that I recommend works of art that are not only beautiful, but also immortal. Because of the technology we all enjoy today, I would like you to connect any time possible, with a source of music and listen to the piece of music I recommend with that particular therapy. I hope that you will enjoy the experience.

"To put the world in order, we must first put the nation in order; to put the nation in order, we must put the family in order; to put the family in order, we must first cultivate our personal life; we must first set our hearts right."

Confucius - Chinese teacher, philosopher, and political theorist (551-479 BC).

2 - KNOW YOURSELF

In order to achieve the state of peace and happiness we all aspire to, we need to know ourselves profoundly. Periodically we review our situations, but attaining the level of contentment that will allow us to treat ourselves with kindness in all aspects of our lives, and benefit from a Gentle Therapy of our souls, we must have a whole and honest knowledge of who we are.

It is important to know that you ARE UNIQUE; no matter how insignificant you might feel when compared with the infinite universe, YOU are unique.

Your genetic make up is expressed in a particular manner that belongs only to you, not even the same as your identical twin. Out of the six billion people inhabiting our planet, no other person has the same face, body, character or talents that you do, although we all are made basically of two eyes and ears, one nose, and one mouth, and the same amount of limbs and organs. Your body is made of 100 trillion cells, of about 200 different types, the smallest found in the cerebellum of about 4 microns, and the longest reaching from your brain stem to your toe. You are undergoing on average a complete turnover every seven years. This means that you are a new person about every seven years, and have a far better chance to exist, and improve, than a cat with nine lives!

Being aware of our strengths and our weaknesses can allow us to use what we have best among the gifts that nature has graced us with, and improve the traits of character that could cause us to ruin situations and relationships.

We all have to work on some of our habits and reactions, and we have to really analyze them, in particular after some events that bring to surface whatever problems we might have. From that point on, we are able to find ways to deal with those issues, learning from others and choosing what feels right to us.

Why not start a list and review your state of health, family situation, job satisfaction, living conditions, and finances?

How about reconsidering your commitments and your goals in life?

What are your needs? What do you think about your habits and daily routine?

How happy are you, and what would make you really, really happy?

We are here to think big, to hold our dreams high, and know that all is possible. For my intention is to bring you to believe that you can achieve the level of joy you always wanted in all aspects of your life.

Know yourself and what you really want, what you are good at, and where you want to go in life. Have a clear vision of your dreams, and be ready to revise them when conditions change. It is all about making good choices at the right time. Based on one important decision in life our paths can be very different. A bad habit, drugs, alcohol, or gambling, can put us in dangerous spiral of destruction; it can happen even to celebrities, and this kinds of harmful directions will lead anyone to disastrous consequences.

This is why we must think hard and choose well when life makes us face unexpected events to which we need to adapt. But this will only make the journey more exciting.

Know that ultimately you are here to BE HAPPY, to accomplish your destiny of a life filed with beauty and satisfaction, while not harming anyone and helping others to reach happiness as well.

How can Gentle Therapy help you to achieve that? I suggest that we *make a list of wishes* based on the analysis of our character and situation. Then, we go to the next step and *design the situation we want to create in life*. This picture of our needs, preferences, and dreams will be the fabric of what we want to construct and achieve during our existence.

From there we *must pay attention to the way we think, speak and react to things and events*. Starting with our thoughts, we should erase all negativity, fear, stress, and criticism. When sitting quiet, or trying to fall asleep, we have the tendency of "turning the wheels" of recent scenes in our mind and getting even more anxious and concerned by them. When thinking of what decisions to make about a specific situation, we consider mostly the catastrophic outcomes. And when we replay a recent moment lived with other people, we may look for defaults and criticize them.

We must stop this way of thinking and learn how to refrain from this bad and toxic habit.

Instead, *we should always have kind words for the happy moments we surely also had in the day, mentally appreciate all the nice gestures toward us, and find what is valuable or pretty in others*. Feeling good and sending love will quiet anger and resentment, when things did not present to us the way we expected. Practically always it appears that worrying was unnecessary, and later things turned for the best anyway.

Changing the way we look at others and think about people and events will make us more relaxed, more inclined to see the good in the real life, and we will attract positive situations to come our way.

Subsequently, for the events coming along in the future, we should continue to scrutinize the way we handle them. Do we continue to over react, to blame, or jump too quickly to the wrong conclusions? *Gentle Therapy applies here as a tempering factor*, a sensible and prudent manner to avoid making hurried decisions, instead of adding more problems to whatever unexpected facts we might have to deal with. In reality the situation could very well be nothing bad at all, but only something different or surprising, and Gentle Therapy will be applied by learning how to *take the time to think through new situations* to have a clearer and realistic view of it.

Here, being gentle means avoiding adding more problems to a possible crisis, and preventing setbacks. Exploding in anger in somebody's face, or making hasty decisions will only aggravate and slow down the whole process by creating unnecessary annoyance that we will need to resolve. Keeping a clear mind is a learning process and helps us to remain gentle with ourselves, particularly when complications arise. It always pays to remain calm, and life is easier with fewer hard moments.

In the mornings it is good to make the habit of starting with a little time to plan your day and have your first moment of Gentle Therapy. *Fill your day with loving thoughts in all the projects or decisions you want to make*; take also the time to *be thankful for the good things in your life*, the blue sky that might welcome you through the window, the birds you hear singing, the flowers that bloom for your delight and for the shimmering of the sun on every leaf or blade of grass. Remember that you live on this incredibly beautiful planet, a free gift given by nature to us all.

Instead of stressful thoughts, *think also to thank and send blessings to anyone who ever did something nice for you or your loved ones*. You will feel more relaxed, flooding your mind with images of warm moments, and this will make your day easier. When I say Gentle Therapy, I mean being nice to yourself when in stressful moments, I don't imply self-pity and lack of concern, I want you to replace negative, pessimistic thoughts, any anger or hard feelings, with *thoughts of the good aspects of your life* instead. You will start to control your anxiety, and will have a clearer mind to find solutions to the problems at hand.

As the day unfolds, *break the tension periodically* with a pause, and look around, find some nice things that are close to you that you might not have noticed. This habit will be particularly helpful when you run into a difficult person or situation. A quick change in the direction of your thoughts could deflect the stressful moment to a pleasant image, giving you the time to calm down and regain your composure. This works every time, in children as well as adults.

Coming home from work, which most of us have as a daily routine, we start processing at 100 miles per hour all the things we want to accomplish, and again stress could invade us in a blink of the eye. Here again, replace the panic attack by thinking of *the pleasure you find in arriving home*, seeing your husband, children, parents, roommates, pets, no matter who might be waiting for you. If you are by yourself, think of the happy, quiet moments you will treat yourself to and create an entire scenario of what you will enjoy tonight. What relaxed clothes you will change into, what music you will play as soon you arrive, what movie you will watch, or which book you would like to read.

Think that you will have time to review messages, mail and answer back your callers. Know that upon your arrival, any *news, as bad as it could possibly be, will not be solved by worries, and a few months from now you, will not have the slightest recollection of them.*

Never forget how amazing you are and how amazing the life you chose should be. You make the choices, and you will become who you decide to be. It is not about where you come from, nor what your background or your family extraction is; these are things you have no control over, you come into life with no power of deciding who your parents are, social level or place of birth are, as in certain countries one cannot even decide what cast one belongs to; all these are not our choices.

All these elements of our life could be an asset or a major challenge, but what we can control is WHO WE WANT TO BE, and as a result, we are responsible for who WE BECOME on our own.

♫

Music to listen to: consider **Ludwig von Beethoven**: **Piano Concerto No 5, the "Emperor".**

The *"Emperor Concerto"* is Beethoven's last concerto and is a monumental piece of music lasting about forty minutes. Beethoven wrote the Concerto in 1811 and, although it has been assumed that Beethoven dedicated this concert to Napoleon Bonaparte, in reality his loyalty went to Archduke Rudolf, his student and patron of that time. Beethoven treats this concerto almost as a solo piano work, and takes liberties from the strict classical concerto form of the epoch, anticipating and transitioning to romanticism.

This way, the first movement while maintaining the traditional first and second theme, are extremely elaborate. Moreover, the movement starts with an introductory cadenza by the piano solo, in contrast with the classical canons imposing a lengthy introduction of the two themes by the orchestra first. The second movement, although more traditional, is a treasure of romantic expression, searching deep into Beethoven's tormented soul, and through his creative alchemy, brings to the surface pure splendor. The third and last movement has a triumphant character, overflowing with dynamism and confidence. Mozart, who preceded Beethoven in Vienna, after hearing the 17-year-old Beethoven performing, said: "keep an eye on this one. Some day he will give the world something to talk about." Indeed, Beethoven reached immense heights of musical inspiration, and listening to the Piano Concerto No 5, will make anyone feel able to conquer the world!

⚄

I recommend **Vienna, Austria**, where Beethoven lived and composed as the place to dream about while reading this chapter. Vienna is also the place were Mozart, Brahms, Shubert and Strauss lived and performed; Gustav Klimt created exquisite drawings in his unique Art Deco style, and Sigmund Freud introduced a new manner of studying the human psychology.

Vienna is a well renowned cultural center with a strong feeling of royalty, with its imperial palaces, museums and churches, where classical music, theatre and opera events are held year around. Wolfgang Amadeus Mozart said about Vienna that this is "the best place in the world" for young musicians.

Vienna is beautifully located on the Danube River, the largest European River. A surprising fact is that the voting age is 16. One can find there the highest waterfall in Europe, and the oldest Giant Wheel in the Prater, and an amusement park where one can enjoy even a gondola ride.

And while you are transported to Vienna, why not take a stroll through the Schonbrunn Palace gardens? You can also have an unforgettable evening sipping Champagne and dancing the waltz at the beautiful baroque palace in the Stadtpark, under the watch of Johann Strauss II, while an orchestra plays and opera dancers invite the guests to join them on stage.

There are numerous places, churches, or music halls, where chamber music concerts and recitals can be attended, and where the musicians play original era instruments, wearing the costumes of the time the music was composed. The experience is unique, with an exact reproduction of the acoustic and ambience by candlelight.

One can stroll in older Vienna, within the Ringstrasse, and enjoy its pubs and coffee houses, or admire the architectural marvels from the imperial time. Vienna's baroque Cathedral dates from the 14th Century, and many museums contain artwork, but one can also visit a butterfly museum, war museum, or electricity museum.

Since you might be listening to Beethoven's music, the most romantic of classical musicians, know that the famous composer lived in Vienna for 35 years, from 1792 until his death in 1827. Vienna devoted to Beethoven several museums, but one will be surprised to discover that Beethoven lived in more than 60 residences, identified by Austrian red and white banners.

Beethoven's intense concentration when composing music, his restless personality, his deafness which prevented him from realizing the high volume levels of sounds he made at night when composing feverishly at the piano, and the fact that he often lacked the money to pay his rent, made Beethoven be constantly moving.

There are also places where Beethoven liked to take a moment to relax and to walk, and a bust of the composer marks a place called Beethoven Ruhe, or Beethoven Peace. Other memorials are by the Concert Hall on Schwarzenberg Platz. Close to Fleichmarkt (meat market), there is a 500 year-old restaurant, where Beethoven enjoyed meals with other musicians and artists.

When walking in old Vienna, enjoy following Beethoven's tracks. You can run into many places marked with the date and the composition linked to that place, houses he occupied for a short period of time, but long enough to produce incomparable symphonies, concertos, sonatas, or chamber music. And while reflecting on his life, it is impossible not to marvel knowing that such a tormented destiny can be transcended by composing eternal musical splendors.

3 – GOOD THINGS AWAIT YOU

DON'T THINK THAT ALL IS BAD WHEN THINGS GO WRONG

This Chapter will address *how to appreciate, through Gentle Therapy, the good things that are in our lives*, looking around to see with new eyes the great gifts that have been bestowed upon us.

You can only do your best with what you have. Sometimes events turn out differently from what we had initially intended, and this might be for the best. How many times have you looked back and found out that unwanted situations turned out to be a blessing?

How many times do we think that we are in control and planning exactly our future moves? We insist in every way possible for events to go exactly as we planned, and we fight against any deviation from the directions we anticipated.

It is very good to plan and have a clear vision of what we want in our life. What kind of family, friends, profession, social activities, what kind of home we would like to live in, and in what part of the world, and we even plan how many children we would like to have.

Then come the surprises, obstacles, when we are not getting into the college we expected, we did not meet the people we wanted, we did not get the job we dreamed of, nor the income we counted on. We think that everything is bad, that all has been only a lure all these years of intense work and sacrifices, and that the whole world is plotting against us. We have regrets and doubts about our decisions, and we think that hard work goes without reward.

In reality, I always discovered, sometimes the hard way, that something better was in my path. The secret of this whole situation is that we put ourselves, our ego, first, thinking that we are the only makers of the future.

If our situation does not turn out the way we want is because we think that we are alone, no help is to be expected other than our own efforts.

Here is where Gentle Therapy can help you: *start by envisioning your future with all your heart*, in all-possible details, and keep it constantly in your mind. Work towards your dreams, but don't struggle with details and minor upsets; relax and *be convinced with all your might that what is the best for you will become reality, in the best way.*

Then let the higher powers help you! *Because you are not alone*, because you can and should be helped, *you can make your journey so much easier*. Be gentle with yourself, invite prayer, quiet moments of meditation, *send love to your dreams and find peace knowing that so much power is at work for you*. Let the infinite wisdom of the Universe guide you, instead of always trying to find solutions on your own and control each and every single detail. Believing in this awesome power has always been proven to work. Why wouldn't you put it to the test? You will be very surprised!

The events that are intervening unexpectedly are part of the excitement of our existence, and they are part of the surprises we are supposed to experience during this great journey we call our life. We should accept them as gifts marking important moments in our existence. Indeed, we should accept these occurrences as divine interventions of a greater wisdom trying to tell us something we should listen to. It could make us aware of different possibilities, directions to consider, errors to avoid, and ultimately save us time and disillusions.

Awareness of what is coming our way, people that we run into, books, a music we hear, or simple signs that are catching our attention, all could be a simple call to pay attention to something of importance. Even a little accident or scare could represent a sign to alert us that we should be more careful in order to avoid bigger pains or losses.

We all lived through major changes we did not anticipate, we moved to places or changed jobs surprising ourselves by these unexpected decisions, without always understanding why and how all this happened. How many times do we hear someone saying that he hopes only for a quiet, steady life, and goes through restarting a new life over and over again in new places?

"Our greatest glory is not in ever falling, but in getting up every time we do."

Confucius

It happened to me: several times I started a new profession, career, and a new life, without any design or prior intention to do so.

I grew up studying music, dedicating weekends, vacations, and holidays to practicing and competing, trying to improve my abilities to play the harp. When I was young, I always admired my father who was a surgeon, and I have always been fascinated by medicine. Later, my father changed completely his professional occupation, and became a renowned artist. But myself, during my younger years, I was not ready to attend dissections, as it was difficult for me to see blood, or even face people suffering.

After I got married and my daughter was born, I realized that even though I was a highly trained performing musician, I was spending most of my time with household chores, going from dishwashing to playing a solo with the Monte Carlo Orchestra. I was determined to take good care of my family, but our social life, family obligations, and the fact that I was feeling very little understanding of my needs as a musician from my new family, were very hard to reconcile. I could not find time and quiet in my own home to practice, and I felt that all my years preparing me to be a professional musician were replaced by ordinary home activities. I practically felt like dying inside.

But stay with me! Here comes the mystery of what destiny can lie ahead of us.

My then husband's job obligations made us return to Paris, France, and this time I did not even have my work with Monte Carlo Symphony. I was considering, and rightfully so, that if I was accomplished or at least satisfied professionally, everyone in the family would benefit as well. Deep inside me, I knew that I would regain energy and confidence, and would eventually be able to juggle my obligations as a mother and wife, if I could have a professional fulfillment. I was naïve enough to even think that I could always still play the harp, at least for myself!

This is when I had a serious conversation with my father, and I will always be very grateful for his advise and the confidence he showed in me, when he encouraged me to go into medicine. Well, he was right, I became an adult and I was finally ready mentally. The funny thing is that I was not ready for anything easier than medicine! I felt very good about that, and although one can imagine the efforts and the long years of struggle and intense work, while caring for my family, I was elated and went through the Medical University like a breeze. I found that my musical education helped me tremendously with my medical studies that required rigorous discipline, precision, and an analytical mind. All this was already inculcated in me, since music and mathematics have common rhythmical structures, and, as in all performing arts, errors are not allowed.

Time went by, and I was already practicing Sports Medicine, Pain Management, and Mesotherapy in Paris, France, for about three years, and divorced for a few years, when fate decided again to knock down all my well-deserved stability. This happened when Robert, my second husband, entered into my life. He was divorced for many years, with two teenage boys, and he was enjoying his freedom in the City of Lights. As far as I was concerned, I considered that I had had enough disappointments and had learned my lesson by then. I was happy and enjoyed a rewarding professional life, I was attending many cultural events, I had good friends, lived in a great place, and I was determined never to get married again. But never say never again!

Robert and I met through common friends, after Robert had a ski accident and suffered from residual injuries. He heard so many times from Jean, his good friend and neighbor, who was also dating one of my best friends, that he needed to stop complaining and go and see their doctor friend to 'fix' his problems. Well, fixing his injuries was quickly done, all right, but he lost his heart in the process. Shortly after that, Robert started showing up when I was going to plays or concerts with my friends, and he became the most delightful, courteous, and entertaining person around. Who could resist such a charming and handsome southern boy?!

The problem was that we were married a few months later, and Robert had already made plans to go back to the States. I still don't know how and what made me decide to follow him with total confidence, but also with total ignorance of the reality of being able to practice medicine in the USA, particularly when not even speaking the language.

Talking about new challenges and turns of destiny! From there on, and for many years to come, everything changed: I had a new family, two more children or rather two grown boys, to get to know and form a new family with. I started giving French and harp lessons, cooking and doing the housewife work, putting all my heart in it and trying my best to make everybody happy. Shortly after, I added to those activities my preparation for the medical equivalence examinations. Most of the English I learned was from the medical books, and it is no wonder why I made my colleagues smile with my French pronunciation of American terms, when later I enrolled in my Internship. Imagine: "ze caroteed arteree"! Fortunately, my English has gotten better since then.

In order to regain my status as a practicing medical doctor, I had to redo my Internship and I changed my specialty to Physical Medicine and Rehabilitation, which I discovered as my new inclination, and which covers also a good deal of Pain Management for musculoskeletal and neurological conditions. From that point on, another "carrousel" of dizzying activities started between hospitals, night calls, exams, scientific papers to prepare, family to care for, and worries of how to pay bills. And the cycle started again everyday: meals to leave to the children for my days of call, follow their education and extracurricular activities, and more cars to maintain and to insure as they were getting older.

I agonized for many years, not even being sure that I would ever get through the difficulties of a new life and career, and that I would ever be able to practice medicine again. This eventually happened, but it took about eight years to close the cycle. And I realized that without the total support and dedication from Robert, I would not have had the strength, nor the courage to go through these years of struggle. We not only survived all this, but the difficulties made our union stronger. Now we enjoy a more quiet life, children being all married, happy and with good professional situations. I love my medical practice, my patients, and the community we chose to live in, and my husband and I are having the loveliest and closest relationship possible. He still makes me laugh, touches my heart with his tender attentions, and he is the best companion to go anywhere with, especially on vacation.

"The gem cannot be polished without friction, nor man perfected without trials."

Confucius

So, one would wonder, why do we go through radical and unexpected changes in life? Why do we have to struggle again, when we were the most comfortable, thinking that we are finally living the way we always wanted?

It is an open and difficult question, but my conclusion to this is that going through hardship, new experiences, or facing unusual choices, will give us the opportunity to grow in life. It could be a "make it or break it" kind of situation, but if we overcome the difficulties, when we have won the challenges and we stand on the top of the mountain, we understand that it was for a greater cause, and it was worth it. Sometimes we lose a situation, that could have been bad, and the changes coming along are for our very best, even though at the moment we feel like broken, and we hang on desperately to the past.

ANALYZE YOUR SITUATION

Let's say you are facing some moments that create some confusion or dissatisfaction in your life. Applying the principles of Gentle Therapy will teach you *first not to panic, and then not to look for the guilty person.*

A good habit to make is to not over react on the moment, but to *find a quiet place and take a moment to reflect on the matter at hand.* But first, make sure you gave yourself enough time to calm down, and learn to start any moment of meditation by creating a feeling of love and peace. Be convinced that, no matter what, nor how big the problem might be, there is always a solution. Ask yourself if you will remember it in five years, or even in one week?

Once you are tranquil, you will have a clearer mind to analyze the situation. Being gentle with yourself will help you to have the right state of mind when you review your concerns, and place them in the context of your whole life.

From there, you can prioritize *by the size and by the urgency* of the problem. Setting order in the affairs of your concerns will make you feel already better. See how Gentle Therapy works even when we are dealing with situations we are required to, but we really don't enjoy?

When you feel comfortable with this way of approaching unpleasant events, why not *consider introducing other members of your family to the same process,* and work things out together? It could bring the relationship to a completely different level. Concentrating on solving problems without wasting time can easily keep your focus on finding solutions. Getting frustrated by bad feelings of blame and anger, all triggered in reality by the anxiety of that particular problem, will only complicate and delay the solution.

Part of the Gentle Therapy technique is understanding that we might not solve the problem right away, or find the solution to the problem on the spot. When calmly reflecting on the issue, *if we don't know the answer immediately, it is fine;* it is much better to let it settle a little longer, and given time the answer might come by itself. It will be a much better resolution to that particular problem when we *look at its different aspects, consider different possibilities, and even get advice from other sources.*

When you have solved a problem, make the habit to recognize it, feel good about yourself, and give thanks to whoever helped you. It could be a simple prayer, but it will bring peace into your spirit, and you *can move on with your life confident, appreciative, and satisfied.*

What you want to obtain from using Gentle Therapy is simply creating those calm and soft moments prior to analyzing a situation. Taking the habit to *face any problem only when you are able to control your emotions.* Go through the selection of priorities, solutions, and, in the end, take a moment to relax and enjoy the good outcome.

The results will be a good feeling of achievement without drama, for learning how to control those chaotic events, ultimately *achieving clarity of mind, order, and peace in your life.*

Other situations that might occur at times are disruptions or unwanted interferences in your life by relatives, friends, or acquaintances. It could be irritating and waste your precious time; again, try to stay calm and don't let it become a dramatic issue. Apply what you already know, give the time to *consider the problem on your time and on your terms*. It could very well be just another nuisance that is not worth your effort, and after reflection you might realize that it will be without consequence in the future.

Gentle Therapy will help you find the real value of the intrusion, which could be only a storm in a glass of water. From here we learn that it is important to choose our battles.

CHOOSE YOUR BATTLES

Life can be full of interruptions, events interfering and disrupting our routines and our plans. At times it feels like we are marching in place, or that our shoes are sticking to the ground. Everything seems to keep us stagnant, without letting us get things done the way we planned. If this happened at work, we would slowly build up mental fatigue and become frustrated or disconnected from our initial goals.

At home, spouse and children seem not to understand how tired we are at times. We snap at the smallest observation, we are irritated by insignificant details, and we feel, oh, so sorry about ourselves.

Now it will be more important than ever to have Gentle Therapy come to our rescue. Reaching the calm and patience required constantly in life when dealing with tensions, will demand *developing the habit of slowing down and taking the time to see the situation more collected.* Making a pause, abstaining from reacting right away, will give us the time we must take to consider how important the whole situation really is. To achieve this level of control over our reactions, we must obtain a degree of *mental silence and quick isolation, while we retrieve the facts and place them at their level of real importance.*

It will require practice, but once this becomes almost a reflex in the way we behave, it will be of extreme benefit for the quality of our life.

The way to practice control over discomfort, can be to simply de*flect our attention toward something pleasant and close by,* an object, or a sound that can automatically sets our mind in a different disposition.

Later on, we could learn how to smile and completely disarm the other person, for anyone will respond happily to a friendly expression.

After giving a little more time to ourselves to reflect to the simple or complicated issues we are dealing with, we realize many times that there is no or very limited substance to our worries. Making a habit to think back and acknowledge that, indeed, it was a good idea not to jump into hasty conclusions will *reinforce our habit of judging first and acting after.*

And all this is obtained by simply being gentle to ourselves.

When coming home feeling drained and tired, looking for someone to take our frustration out on, refrain! Take the habit to think about something happy, put on some music, kiss your spouse, your kid, your pet, or simply send kisses to a flower. If you have any energy left, dance! Laugh, prepare a funny story you want to remember to tell, instead of blasting some reproaches to the other one, (the lazy one), about some matters not being taken care of.

Arriving home, if someone is waiting for you in a bad mood, do the same thing; divert your attention to something pleasant, or let the other one vent. This could be the right time to show compassion and reassurance to the other, when you say that you care, and you mean it.

Gentle Therapy is also when you are *not jumping into every single fight*, and it is also when you don't want to win every single battle. Choose your battles selectively, only for what is really important or vital to you. Choose wisely; let minor upsets go without creating drama, otherwise your life will be a constant boxing game.

Instead, learn to use humor, turn somebody's bad attitude into a laughable matter.

DEVELOP YOUR SENSE OF HUMOR

Breaking the tension with a good joke shows sense of humor and intelligence, making everyone feel more relaxed. The same gentle approach is great in relationships; nothing like a couple that develops over time their own ways of treating problems with humor.

Learning to laugh at our own mishaps or turn somebody's "faux pas" into an unintentional amusing diversion could make any group of people see that a little mistake can easily become a spontaneous moment of entertainment.

We can teach our children from their young age that along with play come stumbles, and a little self-deprecation is a happy way to deal with bruises and scratches. Grown people's bruises and scratches may be harder to deal with, but the habit of seeing the funny side of all situations can make it so much easier to get over them. Again, here we apply Gentle Therapy, and we find a softer way of getting through tough times.

If we look hard, we find that funny moments occur spontaneously in nature all the time, and that can become a pleasant way to entertain ourselves. Observing the birds and wild or domesticated animals the way they interact, can bring us great moments of delectation or sweet emotions. Watching the "Planet's Funniest Animals" is an endless example of tender and hilarious moments, when our little friends can make us forget all worries.

Taking the time to look around and connect with nature makes us more aware of the presence of so much play and happiness that surrounds us, and can constantly keep within us those gentle feelings we try to have always present. And it makes us be a child again!

Learning how to laugh during difficulties is a great way to face adversities and overcome them.

LAUGH OFTEN, LAUGH A LOT, LAUGH EVERY TIME YOU CAN

We've all seen and heard people using laughter as a major weapon against adversities.

Part of therapeutic techniques recommended during major illnesses to enhance the healing process, is laughing a lot, forcing the use of happy images.

By extension, Gentle Therapy encourages you to *use laughter as a major medicine of daily happiness.* It is medically proven that visualization of happy moments from the past, or projected as a wish in the future, feelings of wellbeing and laughter, stimulate the immune system and promote quicker and more complete healing.

Cancer patients watch comical movies, cartoons, and funny shows that make them roar with laughter, shed tears having as much fun as they can, instead of crying from sadness.

I always learned so much from people afflicted with disabilities and finding ways to welcome every happy opportunity and having so much joy in the simple things in life.

I have relatives caring for their young daughter who sustained a brain injury as a teenager. Going through monumental difficulties and major changes in their way of living, they cultivated a great attitude for dealing with every day duties, day in and day out, without complaints, and always keeping a smiling face. Because of their positive attitude, they laugh a lot, and every time they visit, we have the greatest time. Quickly their daughter Carolyn sets everyone in a good mood, and we start making the most hilarious jokes. She is the center of everyone's attention, at home as well as when going out. The joy to see her laugh at the dolphins jumping and playing close by during a boat ride, priceless! By the time they are leaving, we all have had the most delightful time, with the only regrets having to say goodbye.

This is such an enlightened example coming from people that have all the reasons to complain, showing that all situations can become what we decide them to become. We can deal with adversities in a way that we make ourselves miserable, or we transcend them by seeing what goodness lies in those situations.

In all tragedies there are lessons to learn; first we see that things could have been a lot worse, then we look at why and how this dramatic change will affect our way of living. Then, we *learn how to bring the best out of ourselves, growing into someone better and stronger.*

We learn that laughter can be used in all situations, and is a terrific weapon particularly when dealing with misfortune and depression.

So, go out on a limb, and laugh, laugh, and get silly, as often as you can; it is good for your morale and your health!

ENJOY THE FREE GIFTS

There are so many good things out there, and they are free!

I noticed that the most appreciative people are the ones that encountered the most difficulties in life. People who don't take anything for granted have a good sense of value of things, working hard for what they have, and showing gratitude for what they receive. Mostly, they are a good inspiration for how to appreciate the many free gifts that our existence is filled with.

We are surrounded by beautiful gifts of nature, constantly changing seasons deploying its splendor, delighting our senses with beauty. It is good to see the value of what is around us and offered for free, especially when we have limited means, and when we want to stay away from a fast growing consumerist society.

Learning how to observe the presence of even small touches of nature in the middle of the town, can easily take away the pressures of the fast pace of city living. Cutting through a park, or frequently going in the nature, can help us *find the quiet time we all need to restore ourselves, and it keeps us grounded with the wholeness of being part of a bigger picture.*

It is so wonderful to remember the Universe by gazing at the stars, and to appreciate and love this fantastic planet we are living on, with the free wonders that it contains for us to discover.

One can stay in touch with nature practically at anytime, and enjoy looking at any flower, wild or planted, trees, birds, or landscaping. Any animal or plant, as small as this could be, remains a source of wonder for anyone. It is a great idea to have the *children watch some of the many scientific free programs about the Universe, Planet Earth, or the mysteries of nature. This will develop the habit from their early age to discover the place we live in, appreciate it, and love it by staying connected with the nature.*

Just walking in a forest, a park, or a garden, is the best and the gentlest therapy one can have, the best restoration of our soul at anytime.

As I am writing at this moment, we are having the season of the Monarch butterfly migration and mating before the winter, and I am delighted watching them covering my bottlebrush trees, enjoying the last perfect temperature of the fall under the concert of the birds. I can't wait for the hummingbirds to be next on my bottlebrush tree, since these trees seem to be the best and the safest in which to have butterflies, bees, and small birds. It is a reminder of Heaven, and I will not want to miss any of the splendors brought by every change of the seasons.

Recently, I was listening to one of my patients, very distraught about having a hard time keeping her budget on a shoestring. Trying to help her, I suggested her to go into the nature and collect leaves, branches and flowers, and make them into decorations that she could use in her home and sell them as well. Right away she remembered having done this in the past, and becoming enthusiastic, decided to make baskets, scarecrows, ornaments, and wreaths before Halloween.

The ideas kept flowing, and plans were made to have the children be also a part of the fun, and then continue with the celebrations all year long, using the fashion that the nature displays continuously.

I even remembered a simple recipe making small pies from pumpkins found in the fields; cut in halves and removing the seeds, adding a little brown sugar, maple syrup, butter and raisins, then baked in the oven, will make a delicious and earthy desert for the whole family to enjoy and celebrate the Fall. Even the seeds can be seasoned with salt, sugar, or other spices, and eaten instead of popcorn.

But the free gifts are not ending there; in our society we are surrounded by endless activities that can keep us interested and connected with our community. There are libraries where books and videos are free to public access, as are computers, lectures, and a variety of classes. This is another good habit to develop in our children, teaching them to absorb more knowledge from these places of culture, while staying away from the bad influences roaming on the streets.

There is also a whole variety of celebrations for holidays, anniversaries, or local activities, all free and exciting. Boating races, parades of all kinds, fishing contests, Christmas decorations, to name only a few of them.

There are also free concerts given by reputable artists in concert halls, churches, or on the lawns; expos, book signings, conferences, and inaugurations, can all be part of thrilling moments we share with our neighbors, never getting bored, nor feeling isolated. This can also help us know more about the history of our region, the people living or having lived on the same land, their customs and their achievements.

🚲

The place I would like to recommend to visit is the **Loire Valley**, or **Vallée de la Loire**, and in particular its castles. This will be only a quick introduction of this splendid region, since much can be said and a whole book can be easily written about it. A visit to the *Loire Valley* represents a foreword to French culture, its language, architecture, history, and lifestyle.

The *Loire Valley* is part of the *World Heritage Sites*, and is considered as the *Cradle of the French Language* and the *Garden of France*. It is an entire region, spanning over 170 miles following the Loire River in the central part of France. Its mild climate assured an attraction for human establishments since the Paleolithic period, and later its location close to Paris, made this region appealing to the kings of France to build their lavish "secondary residences." *La Vallée de la Loire* with its microclimate conditions offers an ideal place for orchards, produce gardens, thriving vineyards producing famous wines such as Sancerre and Pouilly-Fume.

Many attractive towns grew around the castles with the same names, and the tour of Amboise, Blois, Chinon, Saumur, or Tours can be a great experience.

The kings of France started building castles on the fertile valleys of Loire as early as the 10th century, and today this area accounts for more than 300 castles. First they were elevated as fortifications for defending summer dwellings, (Montbazon, Loches) but with time, a cultural trend developed. The interaction between local villages and land culture, and the architectural sophistication of the castles with their parks and gardens, contributed to creating an exceptional French cultural heritage.

The visitor will enjoy the great beauty of these architectural monuments strolling through historic towns or Chateaux like Amboise, Chenonceau, Chambord, Blois, Cheverny, Chinon, Azay le Rideau, and others. Each castle has a particular design and historical background; for instance, Chenonceau built in 1513 hosted Charles VIII, Louis XII, and Francois 1st. Legendary characters such as Diane de Poitiers, Louise de Lorraine, and Catherine de Medici inhabited Chenonceau, known also as "the castle of six women."

Diane de Poitiers seduced with her beauty Henry II at his arrival as King of France in the middle of the 16th century, although she was 20 years older than him. The story goes that Diane's beauty remained untouched late into her 70s until she died. However, at the death of Henry II, Catherine de Medici made her rival Diane de Poitier leave Chenonceau which she adored, and sent her to live in the Castle of Chaumont, not such a bad place, one might say. Catherine de Medici made her point to embellish even more Chenonceau by adding parks, ponds and bridges, and filling the castle with expensive and beautiful artwork and furnishings, some still decorating the castle's rooms even today.

Chambord is the vastest of the Castles on Loire Valley, with 440 rooms, introducing the taste for places like Versailles. It is one of my favorites, with a grandiose vista at the end of the main alley, as a glorious image of the Renaissance style. The project of the castle started in 1516 at the encounter of King Francois 1st and Leonardo de Vinci. The king brought Leonardo to France when the artist was in his mid 60s, and entrusted him with the project of Chambord and Romorantin. Leonardo de Vinci died in 1519 in Amboise, another beautiful castle, but not before leaving behind the magnificent plans of Chambord. This included the design of its two-way, double helix staircase for Chambord. The royal castle exhibits superb apartments, reception halls and ballrooms, terraces, and parks.

Chambord hosted Moliere who wrote "Monsieur de Pourcegnac" and "Le Bourgeois Gentillhomme" and had the musical support by Lully, during a stay at the invitation of Louis the XIV. There is a long list of important people having stayed or visited this unique place.

Nowadays a visit to the Loire Valley is made simple and exciting. You can choose from many accommodations offered from staying in a castle room with full bed and breakfast, or just dinner and a guided tour. Festivals will invite the visitor to concerts, art exhibits, plays, and Light and Sound shows. One can enjoy attending some culinary demonstrations, or stopping for a vineyard or cellar visit. Flying an air balloon can be done, and coming from Paris directly by helicopter and admiring the splendid view from above the Valley, can be an unforgettable experience.

♫

Music to listen to that I recommend for this chapter is the ***6ᵗʰ Symphony*** **by *Ludwig van Beethoven, "The Pastorale."*** This is one of the pieces of music I love so much; it transports me into the nature and makes me sing along every time I hear it. This symphony was completed and performed in Vienna in December of 1808 and has nature as a theme. It has a "programmatic content", inspired by the composer's walks in the country side of Vienna, and one can envision a peasant dance, the song of a the cuckoo and nightingale, the sound of an water fall, or a storm.

The originality of this peace of music resides in short motives linking playful images of nature with the different movements, appearing from the beginning to the end, and creating a unity of the Symphony. Beethoven shows in this composition not only his love for nature, finding refuge from his troubles by strolling in the woods and along the rivers, but he also finds inspiration from listening to its sounds and tonalities. Beethoven expresses his feelings of great sensibility, illustrating the pastoral life in sounds.

It is even more touching to listen to Beethoven's *Pastorale Symphony*, knowing that soon he was no longer able to hear the real sounds of the nature, but could only reproduce them in his mind, when he became afflicted with deafness at an early age.

4 - YOUR HOME, YOUR SANCTUARY

Everyone's home must be HOME, SWEET HOME, since this special place represents from the beginning of time the place of protection, replenishment, and rest. No matter how modest or how grandiose, from a humble dwelling to a palace, the place we call home is our nest of safety, our cocoon where we hide from the constant invasion of an often harsh reality.

My father used to say, "Man sanctifies the place." That made me believe that one's home is one's sanctuary. Over the course of history, people traveled faraway to find the right place to settle, which they considered as their chosen land. Each family carried a simple object, symbol of their identity, which was placed in a unique area of their new home. It was important to mark and consecrate their habitat as their earthly sanctuary. From there, everyone would decorate and embellish the place in an infinite number of ways, according to their cultural origin.

People carefully selected the sites for their ceremonial structures, where they built temples, burial monuments, or memorials.

The beautiful and majestic Cathedral of Notre Dame de Paris, for instance, is built on top of several layers of religious establishments. There was initially a massive Merovingian structure in the fourth century, that later became Saint-Etienne. Before even the Christian era, on the same site existed a Roman temple to Jupiter. In 1160, Bishop Sully assumed the title of Bishop of Paris, and decided to have a Parisian church constructed that would be "worthy of the kings of Europe." The construction was started in 1163, during the reign of Louis VII, and was completed around the mid 1240's, but embellishments continued through 1345.

Today, Notre Dame de Paris still represents not only a beautiful architectural monument, but also the focal point of Catholicism in France, a place of religious and cultural events; it is the most visited and popular monument in Paris and in all of France, and accounts for more visitors a year than the Eiffel Tower. It makes one think that some places have been destined to hold sacred edifices.

I have always been impressed by the efforts and attention people give to their habitat, according to very large or very limited means.

In Crete, a Greek island, the Palace of Knossos, built around 1900 BC, could contain 10,000 people, which represented probably the entire Minoan population living in the island. At the peak of its glory, Knossos, the capital of Crete built by King Minos, included 1,000 rooms, enjoyed the comfort of an elaborate drainage system for cold and hot water, flushing toilets, underground apartments, and paved roads. Queen Megaron's bath still shows vestiges of frescoes on the walls and exquisite mosaics on the floors, and her alabaster bathtub is waiting for her in case she will come back for a relaxing soak.

Another time, in an isolated village in the mountains of Atlas, Morocco, I was moved by the simplicity of a dwelling where the desire to create a pleasant setting was the same as more fortunate people. In a small hut covered with clay and sitting on simple dirt floors, a young couple just moved in after their marriage. They showed us with so much pride and happiness their abode, where, after we entered it practically crawling inside, we discovered despite the extreme poverty of the place, that the walls were covered with clips from magazines displaying gorgeous landscapes and interiors from around the world.

It was their way of dreaming being surrounded by beautiful settings, and creating within their modest means their own ambience.

Other times, in my travels to the Far East, I was surprised to see that even nowadays, so much importance is still given by large business companies to the details of the location and relations of future buildings with their surroundings. I was amused to observe that the front door of an important bank in Hong Kong was built at a skewed angle with the rest of the building's façade in order to respect the "good magnetic waves" dictated by Feng Shui.

Farther out, on the cliff side of the road is situated a modern concrete high-rise construction replacing one that was barely finished. The story goes that the company formed by Chinese and British members, during a meeting of the Board of Directors, the Chinese counterpart complained that the initial building did not respect the traditional Feng Shui design. It was argued that the company will do greater business if the new building allowed the Mountain, the Dragon representing Strength, to communicate freely with the Sea, representing the Liquidity or Money. So, the initial construction was torn down, replaced by a new one, offering a large square opening of several stories, allowing the financial flow to reach inside. Indeed, it is been reported that the company grew to an unprecedented level of success after that, and the building in question can be seen when traveling on the coastal side of Hong Kong.

In Bangkok, across from our hotel, on the other side of the river, the opening of the new Meridian Hotel was delayed by more than a year, because the master Feng Shui readings were very specific as of the luckiest date and hour for the opening. Needless to say that the orientation and the placement of the hotel were also chosen with respect to the best magnetic currents.

Introducing Gentle Therapy into our home is part of making this place our castle, our Inner Sanctum, our living Sanctuary.

It will be good to start by *leaving all worries outside of the house*, and prevent any negativity to enter. Consider *making your home Your Temple, inviting God or any Higher Power you believe in, to bring in the Light, to cleanse your place, and sanctify it.*

Then, just by *keeping it clean and organized, one already establishes harmony and creates a healthy living space.* The real Feng Shui, which represents an ancient Chinese form of aesthetics, can be used in a more personal way by filling the rooms with good light, and by placing the objects and furniture in an arrangement that gives us comfort and pleases our eyes.

Making our home as beautiful, warm, and serene as we like, we can make it our own kingdom by adding a personal touch, such as a painting we made, a photo we took which reminds us of a special moment, a souvenir or a gift that has a unique meaning.

Our home is a constant working project, growing and changing with us. It reflects different stages in our life, from being a child, then an adult, and growing into an old person. It is the place where we start a family, a place containing so many hopes and dreams. A place filled with high energy, and frantic activity where children are growing. A place where we celebrate birthdays and holidays, where family and friends reunite.

Home is also the place where quiet times come, even if we were longing for them when we were young and very busy. It is the place we need when we want to settle and readjust, when the children leave and the empty nest feeling sets in.

When we look at these steps in life, we realize how well all this is planned. When we are young and bursting with energy and confidence, we are able to juggle career, family, and social activities. Then comes a time when we are happy to slow down, to reflect on what and how our life is, and to which places it has brought us so far.

Our home grows and evolves with us, according to the stages of our life. One can expand it, transform it, redecorate it, or simply change completely the location by moving somewhere else. How excited we are visiting the new homes our children acquire, how happy we are when proudly they show us around; how special is the moment when we contemplate the renovation we made on our dwelling, or when invited to admire the ones made by our friends!

Our home is a reflection of our personality, aesthetic choices, and the history of our life. And a home usually represents the most important acquisition we make in our lifetime.

True, we might slow down as we age, but because we also accumulated so much more experience and wisdom, we are not disconnected from the younger members of our family. We can pass our knowledge on to the next generations, so they can use our experience, and the cycle of life continues.

But until then, Gentle Therapy would suggest that you can start by opening the door holding a bouquet of flowers, no matter if they were picked in the fields on your way home, from your garden, or the florist. Just smile, and bring more beauty and fragrances inside.

Relax, put on some nice music, and *let the house speak to you. Make the habit to spend some time in each room once in a while. Bring in your happy thoughts, and give blessings for what you have. Observe and feel each of these spaces,* try to imagine what would make them more pleasant, so you can establish more harmony.

Inside the house, as out in the nature, *find a favorite place* that allows you to isolate yourself from the usual trepidation of daily activities; a place to be by yourself, find peace, and time for reflection. Make this place your refuge, where you can sort out problems, find answers to your troubles, or simply relax. And don't forget to allow all other members of the family to have their special quiet place as well.

It is good to know that we all can learn how to *transform every simple moment into a special one*. A meal, for instance, can be a delight, even preparing a simple recipe, but with a little imagination, anticipating the pleasure of the others, adding new flavors, and cooking with LOVE. All this represents applying the principal of Gentle Therapy, which in addition of bringing us happiness, enables us to share it with others.

I learned a long time ago that just by making breakfast, lunch, or dinner, I could transform any simple meal into a celebration, if I don't let routine, fatigue, and boredom ever interfere with these enjoyable moments.

All depends on our choices: either complain about having to cook, again, or decide that you will make another happy occasion for your company, family, or friends.

Make things simple, let them fall spontaneously into place, listen to some music, and let it be if things are not always going the way you planned them. It actually can create some very funny situations, those you actually will remember. And keep in mind to not get disturbed unless there is a true catastrophe.

Place the table facing a nice view if possible, use your best china and silverware, (I always do); they are there just for that: make your life more enjoyable, even when feeding nourishment into your body, the way you do it, can also feed your soul.

All this is *applying Gentle Therapy in simple acts of daily life:* enjoying the smell of a stew, barbeque, or a freshly baked apple pie.

Another pleasure around the house is planting a garden or simply keeping a few flowerpots close by. It is so therapeutic watching the results of your production grow!

Getting our hands dirty, connecting with our piece of land, is as restorative as any psychotherapy session, and it is always available at our doorsteps. In addition, it can delight our senses. We can follow the rhythm of the seasons by planting the flowers we prefer, and later they can follow us in the house. We can also keep an herb garden for their use in our culinary preparations. Nothing is fresher than picking up garden herbs as we need them, when making a salad or a dish.

Some people are gifted with a green thumb, and can grow a variety of vegetables, others create amazing designs with shrubs, pergolas covered with wisteria, or walls of bright rose patches. We can also use the turning leaves as indoor decorations, grow lavender and use the flowers in fragrant pillows as a natural home remedy for headaches, or helping to lower the blood pressure and muscle tension. We can make herbal teas from a variety of home grown herbs, such as mint, verbena, and even thyme (known for disgorging the liver).

Then, what a pleasure it is picking fruit from your garden, having them on the table for healthy snacks, ready for baking the pie of the season, or making home grown organic jellies and preserves. We are happy to taste the products of our land and proud to offer our special recipes.

Around the house we maintain our yard, we spend a lot of time tending the lawn and shaping the curb appeal, giving here, too, a little touch of our personality. Competitions are held in the neighborhood, and there is so much happiness and pride in the eyes of the people receiving their seasonal reward, when my husband who is in charge of this pleasant duty of the community, comes to the selected home to present the sign of recognition.

You can also *create your own home spa*, with simple bubble bath, a few candles, and soothing music. There are so many different ingredients that you might want to try, a variety of new fragrances offered in so many places, all intended to relax and pamper you. And yes, YOU ARE WORTH IT, YOU DESERVE IT! Gentle Therapy is also a little R&R ones in a while.

Many couples learn how to give a massage to each other. Even if not very skilled, they *know the benefits of relaxing at home*, and not having to spend a lot of money for that. You have the advantage of keeping your robe and not having to drive back home in a busy traffic. I always have my best night sleep when my husband gives a gentle kneading to my sore muscles.

Home is the place where we celebrate the most important events and holidays, and it is the place we fill with our happiest memories.

For me, Christmas is the best time of the year of all the moments shared by families. Christmas is the time when young and old get together, when gifts are exchanged or feverishly expected as special order directly to Santa, when decorations can get more extravagant then one can imagine. It is the magical time when we believe in mystery, when children behave, and wish Santa Claus a good journey coming from the North Pole and bringing gifts in his sleigh pulled by flying reindeer, to be delivered through the chimney. Christmas is the enchanted time when adults feel like kids, when everyone is forgiven for whatever misbehavior, and when delicious flavors fill the rooms.

Christmas represents for millions, the birth of our Savior, and the hope of humanity for eternal life.

🚲

The place we are visiting in our journey related to this chapter is **Bethlehem**, where it all started.

Bethlehem means house of bread in Hebrew, and house of meat in Arabic. It lies on a hill, five miles south of Jerusalem, and its history goes far back in time, several generations present and recorded by the Old Testament, to the time the Prophet Samuel anointed David as the King of Israel. Joseph, who was from the branch of David, came with Mary, his betrothed, to register in Bethlehem, the town of David, at the decree of Caesar Augustus, who ordered a census of all the subjects of the Roman Empire.

While Mary and Joseph were there, the time came for Mary to have her child, but because of the census, they could not find a room at the inn, and Mary gave birth to her son in a stable, wrapped him in swaddling clothes, and place him in a manger. Since that event, Bethlehem has become sacred to the hearts of millions of Christians, and it marked the transition between the Old and the New Testament.

In Bethlehem there are a number of old houses built over limestone caves. These caves are similar to the cave of the Nativity, and probably Jesus was born in one of these caves rather than in a stable of western tradition.

The Old Testament talks about the prophesies of the birth of the son of God, and Luke describes the signs announcing the event: *"And there was in the same country shepherds watching and keeping the night watches over their flocks, and behold an angel of the Lord stood by them, and the brightness of God shone round about them. Fear not for behold I bring you good tidings of great joy, for this day is born to you a Savior, who is Christ the Lord".* St. Matthew's gospel recalls the visit of the Magi to Bethlehem: *"We have seen His star in the East and have come to worship Him... And Io, the star went before them, till it came over the place where the Child was."*

In the year 135 AD, Hadrian completely surrounded the cave of the Nativity with a temple dedicated to Adonis, god of beauty and love. This providential desecration served to preserve the site for the future, when in 325, Helena, mother of Emperor Constantine, converted to Christianity, and visited the Holly Land. Helena built three basilicas: the first over the Calvary in Jerusalem, the second over the cave of Nativity in Bethlehem, and the third on the top of the Mount of Olives.

When the church of the Nativity was built, first was removed the temple ordered by Hadrian, and the cave was found intact. Helena, encouraged by Constantine, then built a magnificent basilica, richly decorated with mosaics, marble and frescoes, some preserved until now.

When I visited the Church of the Nativity, it was so moving to see side-by-side pieces of the original decorations with the reconstructed ones. In spite of the fact that the beauty of the interiors was damaged through centuries, the essential form was not altered, even in 614, when the Persians invaded the Holy Land and destroyed all its churches and convents, the Church of the Nativity was the only church evading the destruction.

The Church of the Nativity has a façade encircled by the walls of three convents. The basilica itself has the shape of a cross 170 feet long, and 80 feet wide. In the upper part of the church, the transept walls still hold some of the mosaics left from the

Crusaders. Below is a beautiful Greek orthodox choir standing above the cave of the Nativity and is hand-carved in wood from cedars of Lebanon.

The cave of the Nativity is below the choir in a rectangular shape, 35 feet by 10 feet, and lit by 48 oil lamps. The original roof of the cave was replaced with masonry to prevent fire, offered in 1874 by McMahon, President of the French Republic.

The Holy Manger is to the right, and a silver star marks the spot where Christ was born, with the Latin inscription *"Hic de Maria Vergine Jesus Christus Natus est."* (Here Christ was born).

This holy place inspires reverence, is filled with a mysterious but real presence defying millennia, giving hope and reassurance to all.

♫

Music I propose: any **Christmas Carols** you like, knowing that you can enjoy them all year long.

Carol, or Carole, is a French and Anglo-Norman word, meaning a dance song, expressing joy of celebration. Before Christianity, Carols were sung in Europe thousands of years ago, as a celebration of the Winter Solstice, and people danced and sang around stone circles. It is believed that Saint Francis of Assisi introduced carols in 1223 instead of formal sacred hymns during the Christmas Mass in Greccio, province of Umbria. Since then, minstrels and troubadours crossing the western land of Europe, entertained people going from home to home, mostly around Christmas time. Nowadays, only the songs survived the tradition as Christmas Carols. Carols were sung in Latin, but also, French, Normand, Spanish, or German. The earliest written Carol known, dates from 1410, and a small fragment is conserved, telling the story of people visiting Mary and Jesus in Bethlehem. Some popular Carols survived the time, like "Good King Wenceslas," or "Once in Royal David's City." But who wouldn't join in for "O come, all ye faithful," "Christ is born in Bethlehem," "Silent Night," or "O Holy Night?"

"God, grant me the serenity to accept the things I cannot change, the courage to change the things I can, and the wisdom to know the difference."

Reinhold Niebuhr (American theologian, 1892-1071)

5 - FINDING PEACE AND SERENITY

In the precedent chapter, we were talking about creating a serene atmosphere in our home. Finding the peace and serenity we all long for in our daily lives is another important part of Gentle Therapy, and it is another challenge we have to face and overcome.

There are two ways to find peace in our life: one is either to find *a place, create a situation, or think of a person that inspires this feeling of peaceful content and brings our mind to calm and balance*. The second is *fighting negativity in our lives,* and to do so, we must eradicate whatever we fear or dislike, purge what makes us feel unsettled, unhappy, or leads us to the brink of a panic attack.

FIND YOUR INSPIRATION

Let us start with finding the right place; every person has a preference for pleasant and beautiful places to visit as often as possible. Some of them are close by, representing some frequently visited refuge, where we can recover our composure, or find precisely the quietude we need. Some others are more remote locations, that we became attached to when visiting them, or are part of dear projects we wish to go to in the future.

Whenever we encounter a place, situation, or we are in the presence of a person that makes us feel good, moves us by its beauty, kindness, or feeling of happiness, we are marked for a longtime, and we hope to sense it again.

The first step in our quest for peace is to find a way to experience again this strong feeling of peace and serenity. Many of us have a secret place, pleasant view, a tree to hug, a song to sing, a friend to call, or a fishing honey hole to visit. We developed the good habit to walk, run, bike, or listen to music, because these activities give us a well being feeling of relaxation, keeping our body in good shape, while clearing our minds from worries.

Any kind of exercise is good, and anyone who has developed the habit to play, stretch, attend a class of yoga, aerobics, swimming, or taking the dog to the park, should continue to do it regularly. And the ones who don't, should start, for these good habits are not only good for our health, but they establish a well deserved balance between working and relaxing.

Another way of introducing in our lives *moments that bring us tranquility is to start by creating or imagining places and situations through quiet moments of meditation.* I am not talking about activities that are enjoyable in the company of friends or family, from playing cards, attending a party, or a football game. All these activities are welcome and pleasant, and nobody needs any kind of special training to have fun.

We are here to talk about how to obtain peace in our lives in a world of constant aggression from stress and fatigue. The more stress and concerns we face in life, the less we feel capable of thinking clearly and dealing rationally with problems. From there it is easy to go down in a spiral of giving up and becoming depressed.

"Peace cannot be kept by force; it can only be achieved by understanding."

Albert Einstein, Nobel Price for Physics, 1921

We already discussed creating our sanctuary at home and finding these quiet moments. Now, it will be good to extend this peacefulness to our lives wherever we are, while *building inside us mechanisms able to restore or obtain peace and serenity at any time.*

So far, we thought about places or situations that make us feel good; my recommendation is to experience them often and regularly. If you don't have such a habit, it will be good to create one: finding a corner in your garden, or going farther out in the nature. There, *start by contemplating your surroundings and relax, pushing away any negative thoughts* that would come to trouble you. In the beginning just quiet your mind, feel the place, look at the trees, leaves, flowers, and admire the light or the starry sky. Furthermore, try to remember this calm you experience during your regular activities, while at work, or driving during the rush hours. Little by little *introduce these moments of mental peace while dealing with any stressful situation.*

Getting to this point, you already achieved a tremendous progress in obtaining control over the events in your life. This will make solving problems a lot easier, you will experience less fatigue, and your health will greatly benefit from less stressful aggressions. Your mind will be less clouded by anxiety, and your judgment will improve.

FACING PROBLEMS

The next phase of Gentle Therapy is to write or think of a list including as many things as you consider serious enough to make you anxious or depressed; one cannot feel peace or satisfaction in life if there are important aspects of one's life disturbing the harmony one desires.

Introduce images and ideas of what will make you happy and what you want to obtain in life. You might want to start by obtaining inner peace, self-esteem, happiness, good health, and prosperity. For you are here to obtain all these wonders in your life, and help good things come your way.

Feeling stressed, ruminating everything negative happening in your day, will only attract negative energy: your magnetic vibrations, as demonstrated scientifically for quite a while, will resonate only to the same type of negative waves, that will continue to surround you. The more you feel pessimistic, the more you amplify the negativity you plunge into.

Let's make a list of these dreadful problems we try to ignore every time we can; this time we will face them straight in the eyes, we make a list, and we want it as long as possible so we don't miss anything, and by writing the problems down we acknowledge them without fear.

Any insecurity, lack of happiness, money, job, satisfaction in relationships, or self-esteem, we write it down. Any feeling of being ugly, fat, unpopular, or getting old, any longing for love and appreciation will be in the list. Anything that makes us feel less, less talented, less funny, less gifted, in a word, 'less' good than others, will be pinned down on the list with the sharp arrows of rediscovered power. This is *the power to recognize what limits us in life and prevents us from living life fully*. By ascertaining our limitations, we found the courage to face them as well, and one should consider this as a liberating step in obtaining satisfaction and harmony in life.

REDISCOVER POWER BY FIGHTING NEGATIVITY

Good; now that we have this infamous list in front of us, let's *match each and every problem with its solution*: for anything that we lack, we write as we already having it. For example, next to lack of love, we write LOVE and HAPPINESS; lack of money, debts or poverty, we will have next PROSPERITY and WEALTH; illness will be paired with GREAT HEALTH; any deprecating sentiments about ourselves will be facing positive physical or character traits: BEAUTY, SELF CONTROL, CONFIDENCE, and RECOVERED ENERGY. Our aspirations will be recognized and marked down: SUCCESS and ACCOMPLISHEMENT; our gifts and talents RECOGNIZED and REWARDED, and the most difficult of all, ANGER or HATRED replaced by LOVE and FORGIVENESS.

After reviewing the list we established, a list that can remain open for additions, corrections, or deletions at any time, we should take every element replacing the problem and reflect on that positive word.

So, let us *start now by controlling our thoughts*. After becoming quiet, emptying our minds and removing the noise of trivial activities, *concentrate on one important aspect of your life that you want to change or obtain.* Soft music or a prayer might help to reach the state of relaxation you need.

SENSE YOUR FUTURE AS REAL

Here, spend a little time, thinking about every positive word representing one goal at the time. We reflect on the feeling *we experience as if we have already obtained that particular goal.* Taking all the time that might be needed, we first imagine that particular sensation, and then, we must experience it with all our might, will all our desire, *as it is for real in our life.* It will take some time to achieve this control of our feelings, but this will be the progression toward *replacing what we have negative in our life with the positive we desire.*

I am aware that some situations are quite difficult to deal with, and turning them into good ones is more complicated. It might help to know that every person has to face one way or the other some serious challenges. Obtaining harmony in life is not only a psychological approach of our feelings; sometimes it means looking into bruises of our soul, as everyone strives to gently restore a wounded spirit.

MAKE ORDER IN YOUR RELATIONSHIPS

A common example of troubled relationships is when dealing with family relations. How many times I hear about a friend or a patient that some members of the family are repeatedly rescued from their mistakes or lack of responsibility. This is creating strain on the same person over and over again, who makes the efforts and hopes that the culpable one will learn and that this will be the last time to provide help. Most of the time, this situation has been built over many years, through a complex history of events. In order to reverse this intricate and thorny relationship, one has to re-establish the foundation itself of this bond.

First, one should look at that particular situation or relationship; are you feeling responsible for what happened to the other one, are you filled with guilt if you don't continue saving that person, are you exasperated continually bailing out someone who does not seem to learn?

Where are you at this stage in your life, are you making efforts to establish a stable and happy life, and are all these disruptions are dragging you down?

If your answer is "yes" to most of these questions, it is an indication that you must stop this pattern, and give a *new orientation to the relations* you maintained until now. Keep in mind that your decision will not only help you to go on with your life, but it will help the other person to take control of his or hers. As long as you constantly resolve one's troubles, why do you think anyone will ever want to break loose from this comfortable relation maintained and deeply imprinted to only one's benefit? And believe me, some people are very crafty when it comes to taking advantage of others. Take it from your own experience, and consider that you are not helping in the end; and it only makes you, in a strange way, feel good. This will prevent the other relative to progress toward his own direction and achieve personal fulfillment.

It took me a longtime to understand that one cannot change another person who is not willing to make changes; going through efforts and heart aches, lots of waste of time showing patience and dealing with intense stress, all these efforts are in reality not rewarded by the other one but by their falling back again into the same lifestyle.

How many times we worried about our parents getting older, needing assistance, and how often not accepting it? Here, there is no perfect recipe as to how to handle disease, lose of independence, even end of life. No matter how old we are, we still the "children" and ought to listen to our parents, and not be the ones giving directions.

In these circumstances, the only thing we can do is to show love, offer assistance financially, or offer our time. This is about all that is within our possibilities.

Patiently show what is available technically or socially that can improve our loved ones' quality of life; it may be moving to a one level house, or installing and using new devices that can make their environment safer, reassuring them that making some changes does not automatically mean going to a nursing home. Encourage them to accept home health from nurses or therapists. Attending community events and socializing with other persons with similar problems or interests, can keep our older members of the family mentally stimulated, physically active, and connected with the rest of the world.

At this point, in my opinion, the best way to apply the Gentle Therapy technique is to decide once and for all to *concentrate on your life, offer kind advice to those who accept it, keep love in your heart for the others, wish them only good, and keep them in your sincere prayers.*

IMPROVING OURSELVES

The ultimate goal in getting to know our most profound and dearest wishes is not only obtaining the good things we want and deserve in life, but this is also a *transforming process*. Mastering fears, anxieties, impulsions, or imperfections can liberate us from blame and shortcomings, and improve ourselves by replacing these traits or feelings with what we have the best to give, becoming the best we can, while maintaining the best and most balanced relationships with people that appreciate us. Understand that you are not going to make everybody on the planet happy, and having your circle of family and friends that counts for you and makes you also happy, is all one can realistically handle and expect.

There is a great satisfaction when achieving something we are wishing for, when we overcome a difficulty, or when we replace a trait of character with the best opposite. This is indeed part of the Gentle Therapy representing the *transforming step of improving ourselves in order to improve our life and achieve satisfaction and peace.*

Once we are aware of the thrill and exaltation that comes with this newly acquired condition of well being, we want to be caring, loving, and bring as much happiness to others as we can.

From this point, *we must introduce this same sensation we experienced while meditating every time the old habits resurface.* We must reflect at how calm and relaxed we were when we replaced stress with tranquility, and we invite those good feelings to take over.

As part of the Gentle Therapy I propose also to *celebrate every time we attain the control over a difficulty, no matter how small.* Not responding to a provocation, turning a tensed ambience into a pleasant one, stopping the first impulse to overreact, all these represent a triumph well earned, and should result in a great feeling, that you should reinforce every time. You know by now that every difficulty is an opportunity to learn how to deal and overcome obstacles, and becomes an experience about how to grow and improve.

What can be a better therapy than this transformation of negative aspects in ones life? *Becoming the best one can be, mastering our feelings and reactions, having the purpose of being as happy, as carrying, and as loving as one can be is the best way to find true satisfaction.* In my humble opinion, this is the way to achieve an everlasting peaceful and serene life.

"Better than a thousand hollow words, is one word that brings peace."

Buddha

♫

Music to listen to: Johann Sebastian Bach, "Concerto for Two Violins" in D minor.

Considered as one of the most famous late Baroque period pieces of music composed by Bach, *"The Double Concerto for Violin"*, or the *"Concerto for Two Violins"*, was written between 1730 and 1731. Extremely expressive in a beautiful gentleness, the musical thread moves as a lace made by the dialogue of the two violins.

I had the immense pleasure to attend a concert with David Oistrakh and Yehudi Menuhin, with Sir John Barbirolli as director. What a dream team! Divine music and divine violin sounds transporting everyone to the highest places of complete, perfect serenity. I was surrounded by the unique sounds created by the magic of the best performers of our time, one playing on a Guarneri violin, and the other on a Stradivarius.

It is interesting to note that Menuhin, a Russian Jewish American living in England and barely escaping the Nazi Holocaust, practiced meditation and yoga to find strength when dealing with stress during those trying times. The friendship between Menuhin and Oistrakh started back in 1945 across the iron curtain and lasted until Menuhin's death. Each one was in admiration of the other, Menuhin was considered as a child prodigy, "the Mozart of the violin," Oistrakh was a giant of the century in the mastery of violin playing. Menuhin did not speak Russian and Oistrakh did not speak English, they communicated in a dialect of German, but they understood each other perfectly through music.

Yehudi Menuhin was one of the first to perform in Germany after World War II, going in 1947 for a reconciliation concert of the Berlin Philharmonic Orchestra with Wilhelm Furtwangler as director.

🚲

Place to visit: Lake Como, Italy.

Lake Como is situated 40 km north of Milan and at the border with Switzerland, and is the most popular Italian lake. It originates from a glacier, and is the smallest of a group of three lakes in northern Italy at the frontier of Switzerland, along with Lake Garda and Lake Maggiore. It is a weekend destination for people from Milan, but at any time visitors from all over the world can be seen around the superb scenery of the lake.

Lake Como has been popular since the time of the Romans, they called the place Comum, and since then, wealthy aristocrats have come and built luxurious villas and palaces.

One can attend some the numerous attractions that this great place has to offer; a music festival is held each summer, boat racing or parades, fireworks and folk festivals, historical re-enactment, or gastronomical fares. There is also a Silk Museum in the town of Como, and many silk factories display their fashionable creations.

There are a variety of outdoor activities such as biking, hiking, paragliding, windsurfing, or skiing, according to the season. Camping is possible in a number of camps around the lake, and there are attractive cruises to choose from. For fishing lovers, the village of Varenna will welcome anyone with its typical charm of narrow alleys, found below the castle.

Everywhere there are multiple paths for leisurely walking, historic centers, lovely squares and cafes, and from anywhere one can admire the calm and mysterious beauty of this enchanted place.

Many beautiful and picturesque towns border the lake, while Bellagio is considered as the pearl of the lake, situated at the confluence of the three branches of the 'Y' shape made by the lake. The Bellagio Casino in Las Vegas was inspired by this exquisite site, and tried to reproduce the magical attraction of the original location.

Besides the beauty of the settings, the towns around Lake Como will tempt the visitor with many activities; for example, in the village of Cernobbio one can visit Villa d'Este, a famous and luxurious villa opened to the public and boasting 161 rooms, each one decorated in a unique design, for an unforgettable stay.

The resort of Menaggio is popular for its pleasant outdoor settings, where swimming, rock climbing, walking, or windsurfing are the local attractions, while Villa Carlotta, more south from there, will display its beautiful gardens.

Villa Balbianello located in the village of Lenno, was a set for one of the "Star Wars" movies, and is worth a detour.

Lake Como was the setting for the James Bond movies, "Casino Royale," and the more recent one, "Quantum of Solace," while Villa Erba served as the background location for "Ocean's Twelve."

There is no surprise why so many celebrities have been attracted by Lake Como. Madonna, George Clooney, Sylvester Stallone, and Gianni Versace found there an exceptional and quiet place to retreat.

"Lord, You have blessed my food and water and have taken sickness away from me. Therefore, I will fulfill the number of my days in health."

(Exodus 23:25,25)

6 - HEALING THERAPY

As a natural progression from learning how to find peace in our lives, comes the need for well being of our body and mind in order to obtain real long-standing harmony. While learning how to meditate on the objectives to attain, controlling our fears and insecurities, we will include now our state of health, with any of the troubles that we might have about it, and with the firm intent to obtain complete and perfect healing.

Wait a minute here! I can hear already your protest, "my problems are beyond just meditating and finding peace of mind." And this is all right, one can need a lot more than that, I will not deny it. Certainly, you will have to *follow closely any and all treatments that you are receiving; this is without any doubt part of taking care of your health, either physical, or mental.* My intention is to make sure that you are not in any way disrupting your schedule nor the routine of treatments you might undergo.

What I intend to do by introducing the idea of a Healing Therapy, is to add a Gentle way that will increase your means to fight whatever illness you might want to defeat.

In truth, my message is to use every bit of what science offers, and combine it with a larger view of approaching disease, including the way we experience it mentally and emotionally. *It is definitely not turning our back to what new discoveries of science and technological advances have to offer, but to embrace them with confidence and optimistic expectations.*

For instance in many types of cancer treatments, newer researches and their utilizations in the cure of even advanced stages, are looking into using our own natural abilities to eradicate the disease. It is wonderful and of a spiritual dimension, although supported by concrete scientific results, to see that our body has been bestowed with everything necessary to restore it to its perfect condition. As an example is using the patient's own line of killer cells extracted from samples of his blood, multiplied in a way similar to growing stem cells, and introduced back into the patient's body, having his own cells destroy specifically the cancerous cells, with no toxic products, no unnecessary damage to healthy tissues, and no side effects!

Likewise, in the treatment of infections we've seen with what rapidity the bacteria and viruses acquire resistance through fast mutations, making the antibiotics soon obsolete. Employing the same principle, researchers found that extracting the molecules produced by our B-cells as antibodies in response to microorganisms attacks, multiplied in cultures, then reinjected into the same patient's body, will offer in the future a highly specific, non toxic treatment. This has also the advantage to provide longer protection against relapses.

Stem cells are another line of treatments promising already great changes on chronic and devastating diseases. Leaving alone the embryos, we are already collecting embryonic stem cells from the umbilical cord or the placenta, tissues that most of the time are discarded, until we learned of the extraordinary potential demonstrated in microbiology, using the stem cells extracted to recreate new tissues and organs. More recently it has been easier to grow stem cells from adults, with additional benefits of using the patient's own cells in order to restore failed or destroyed organs.

Just imagine diabetic patients, and particularly children, who will never need to prick themselves and inject Insulin three or four times a day, no longer restricted in their diet and activities, if their pancreas is restored to its ideal condition. Patients with kidney or any other organ failure will no longer have to wait for dialysis or transplants, endure traumatizing surgeries, and anti reject treatments all life long. The same for paralyzed patients from spinal cord injuries, people affected with Alzheimer's, Parkinson's and other central nervous system disorders, being offered on the same manner complete recovery.

Although this possibility is nearly considered a miracle, we are on the very way of advancing medical therapies close to this era of newer healing techniques. This will bring not only a much more satisfactory outcomes, enabling millions of patients and their families to enjoy a full and productive life, but by providing complete recovery, there is no more need for further treatments, reducing dramatically the cost of health care of the entire nation.

We all must support the advances of science and consider the importance of budget allocated to research. And we all should be reassured when engaging in Gentle Therapy that there are wonderful ways of obtaining a great state of health, relaxing, and opening our beings for good things to come to our rescue, even if we don't always understand the way they work.

I have the strong belief that discoveries and inventions are in reality the products of divine inspirations of great minds dedicated to bringing improvements to the human condition. I am myself a physician, but along with other fellow doctors, I feel that God is there to lead us when we ask for his help, and guides us in our decisions and treatments, for we are only his instruments, and He is the one who heals and performs miracles.

Through positive attitude, abolition of stress, using at any time the techniques of relaxation we are introduced so far, I advise, along with the help of the latest treatments and discoveries, to utilize these additional methods in order to enhance and optimize all our chances of success in fighting illness.

Using science again, we have a vast amount of medical documentation based on multiple and extensive medical studies proving *the healing power of the prayer, meditation, and positive visualization.* This is obtained by stimulating precisely our own healing mechanisms we have been granted with from the beginning of times.

Some recent medical studies bring up the *importance of people's attitude*, and their character in the quality of their life, and their life span as well. Somebody cynical, who represents someone bitter, disappointed in life, and untrustworthy, basically someone miserably unhappy, will live 3 years less than a person with a positive attitude. It is demonstrated also that stress promotes cholesterol plaques building inside arteries, which will lead to strokes and heart attacks, while inhibiting our immune system and making us more prone to infections.

I will not burden my reader with a long list of bibliographic references; it will be more helpful to get started by reflecting on the condition we toil with.

Having already mastered the aptitude to *relax in a preferred place that helps us to unwind, we will slowly bring up the nature of the healing we wish to accomplish*. Then *consider what we want*, completely.

From there, we *define the goal we want to obtain*, keeping it realistic, even if we will need to consider going through multiple steps. We will have fewer deceptions if we anticipate, according to the complexity of the situation, having a long way to go, and we celebrate each small victory, one at a time.

Healing this way will be through *changing the mental attitude toward disease*, and it works by *finding what is blocking the flawless balance in the way our body and mind communicate.* Our whole being is destined to be perfect, perfect in function, beauty, attitudes, and relations, feeling perfectly happy, and perfectly healthy. In order to obtain this level of joyful state, we need to *regain this aptitude of letting the flow of life itself do its perfect work.* This is the work of marvelous physiological functioning, the wisdom of the mind, and the extraordinary ability of healing. It is going back to the original image of self, as we were created and born perfect and pure, from an original cell containing all the knowledge, all the mystery of the creation, and all the wonders of the Universe.

Now we understand that in order to heal, we need to heal the body, we need to heal the soul, and we need to heal the past.

Once we find out what are the medical conditions we are dealing with, and our goals are defined and in place, it is time to *uncover what is blocking us*. There can be bad habits in our life style, situations that scarred us for life and we cannot rid the stress we feel because of it, a past trauma that wounded our souls. All these traumatic experiences have left us scared, sad, angry, and made us lose confidence in others. From there it is only a small step to become negative, to think that nothing good can be expected in life. And these situations are precisely what create blockages in life for the good functioning of our body and mind, and for the good things and events to manifest. Fear, sadness, hatred, jealousy, loss of confidence and purpose, detachment from what life has to offer, all these conditions are interfering with our happiness, and here is where lies the crucial changes that must be made.

During the relaxation and meditation moments, let's consider what are our habits and how do we treat our body. Our body is our temple, unique receptacle containing not only our organs, but also our soul during the journey of this lifetime. It contains our mind, with its ability to elaborate thoughts, process events and solve problems, store new information and retrieve it when needed, plan ahead and make complex judgments to come up with solutions, basically an intelligent mind. It also contain our emotions, ability to love or hate, our dreams, desires and talents, not demonstrated as material organs or tissues, but nevertheless so real, strong, and vital.

"I present my body to God for it is the temple of the living God. God dwells in me and His life permeates my Spirit, Soul, and Body, so I am filled with the fullness of God daily".

(Romans 12:1,2; John 14:20)

We have been, all of us, entrusted with this marvel that is our body, and *we have the responsibility, the mystical obligation to take good care of it, to honor, respect, and keep it in the best condition possible.*

From here, we understand how important it is to review how we treat our body; many of our afflictions can be the consequence of long lasting abuse and mistreatment we've done on our own.

During the time we contemplate the condition of our health, it is important to make the *distinction between the illnesses* resulting from an unfortunate occurrence, or as an end result of our *unhealthy life style*. It is fundamental to understand that if one continues to inflict harm to its body or mind, the reason for suffering will continue not only making that person feel poorly, but the deterioration due to that continuous abuse will get worse. One cannot expect to get better without stopping the cause of the ailment, since the disease is a direct consequence of bad habits and is the origin of becoming ill. So, we must be honest with ourselves and see if there is anything that we need to change in our lifestyle in order to eradicate the problem, as we would do with a virus, bacteria, or any other foreign body.

Through the process of Gentle Therapy we will *analyze quietly, with clear mind, all aspects of the harmful habit or addiction.* Gently, we recognize the destruction that this can cause in our life, the price we sometimes pay, not only with our health, but also with the possible loss of our relationships, employment, financial security, or even our freedom. The next step is to decide to definitely put a *stop to any self-destructive activity, under any form or circumstances.*

From there, *we affirm that we are ready* to discard the old manners and behavior, we meditate or repeat mentally in any situation that we are entering into a new era of our life, an important and wonderful turn for the best. *We repeat this mantra over and over until we are absolutely convinced by the commitment to change* until we feel the happiness of being liberated from the claws of dark experiences, and we actually live and absorb with every breath the new reality.

We will also need to be ready to *accept the idea of forgiveness*, and to be able to let go and move on. It is a matter of choice. But this is possible applying the principles of Gentle Therapy: being gentle with yourself, means learning to like and *accept yourself, it means wanting and becoming someone lovable.* From there, it is easier to *forgive whatever difficulty you bear from the past.*

All things are interconnected; in order to accept the others, to be integrated with the world, you have to start by accepting yourself. You must choose to unload the memory of any hurt, sadness, regrets, or hatred. *Accepting yourself means also getting rid of the poor image you might have of yourself, of any resentment, or guilt.*

> *"Forget injuries, never forget kindnesses."*
>
> *Confucius*

Through Gentle Therapy, you will *learn what is good about yourself*; you will begin to like who YOU are. Cleaning your soul from negative images and thoughts, and replacing them with positive, loving ones, will heal you. These are only images, only thoughts, and you have the power to change them.

Your thoughts become your beliefs, and your beliefs your reality, because your reality is your truth.

Even when we have achieved a happy balance in life is good that periodically we *take an introspective look at how we feel inside* and we refresh the image of ourselves, of our world. Are we, again, falling into the habit of criticism, or anger? Are we becoming ill tempered for minor upsets, or are we thinking that this must be the result of "God's punishment"?

I strongly believe that God has nothing to do with any kind of "punishment." God does not want us to suffer, and He is not a vengeful, punishing God. He is Love, knowledge, and splendor. He is the Universal Power, and He is not judging us, but sending us awesome gifts, to help us on our accomplishments.

If there are wars and violence, humans inflict suffering to other beings, - we do it to each other in a despicable way. And we reap what we sow; *the actions, thoughts that we release into the Universe come back to us – it is as simple as that.*

That is why it is so important to *be careful of what we think, affirm, or do*. It is our choice of the present that decides what we will have in the future. With every thought, every word, every action of the present moment, we decide our future, we set the terms of our happiness or misery, our success or our failure, we bring into our body disease or health.

When somebody does to us a terrible offense, *never wish something bad* to happen to that person; wish only good and turn away, for his own actions will come back to haunt and bring the results of his own doing. *Never load your soul with the bad Karma of someone else's evil actions.*

Let's now talk about some of our bad habits, and start with *eating habits*. Eating is not only a way of sustaining our body with the nutrients needed for survival, but also it became a natural opportunity of showing hospitality, or enjoying special times with loved ones. And all this is alright, we should consider our meal time as a celebration and not as a way of filling up as much and as fast we can with the food stuff. Any over doing in any occasion is bad for us, and this is an adage known since the world exists. Too much food, or too much starvation, represent extremes resulting in serious unbalance in the way we treat our body; we are aware of the devastating consequences of obesity as well as anorexia, conditions that can ultimately lead to our demise. Which brings in the idea of MODERATION. In all we do in life in order to really enjoy good things, we need to be reasonable, never going of the balance.

When dealing with an over weight condition, in some occasions there is a medical reason resulting from hormonal imbalance and this condition needs to be treated accordingly by a specialist. It could be that some people will "burn calories" less fast, meaning their metabolism is slowed down, while others are naturally fast metabolizers. Our genetic mapping varies from one person to another, and not every one is equal in this matter, and it IS so unfair!

However, we all experience periods of higher or lower metabolic speed, and the weight does not always reflect our metabolic index. As an example, models have in many cases a high body fat index especially when they are very thin, and this is because too much fasting causes their body to slow down to a starvation mode in order to save the little amount of food ingested.

I once had a patient who had terminal metastized cancer and his wife decided to save him by finding a cure through some "new age" treatments, taking him completely off all medication and starving him. Her idea was to kill the cancer by not providing nourishment to malignant cells; she might have killed the cancer, all right, but she was, with all good intentions, killing her husband in the process.

As a contrast to abstinence from food, is an interesting phenomenon observed in some countries under the communist regime, where the quality food was scarce. Women were rather overweight, although for the long winter months the only food available was potatoes and some cabbage. The reason of their 'puffiness" was from the volume ingested to make them feel full, but in reality potatoes have very few calories, and the nutritional value was very small (used in some diets today, in order to cut down on calorie count). Thus, calorie count is not always the most important element to watch, since there are calories and calories, potatoes might bring you the false impression of cutting down on your intake, it might fill you up and chase away the hunger, but you will have a very poor energetic value of your food, and this can add inches to your waist-line.

In America we are mostly dealing with obesity. We observe a new social condition where people are obsessed with working out and are still overweight more than in any other nation in the world.

Obesity as the direct result of over eating is where we must take control of this dangerous habit. I know, we always come up with some excuses: too much stress, too much temptations, weddings, receptions, the Super bowl, Christmas holidays, excuses, excuses. Obesity can be another example of extreme eating habits we must avoid.

Here we have to *come with a plan*: get all the information about what is available in choosing a healthy eating basic program, establish our goals, and get started. There is a common knowledge that in addition to healthy choices of food we need to include an exercise program, and understand that losing weight and keeping it within a reasonable average, means staying healthy.

This book is not a diet book, and if needed, I recommend the reader to research among many wonderful writings or watch some good TV programs that are very informational.

I will address only a few basic notions about keeping healthy eating habits, which I will not call diet: one is *avoiding too much salt or too much sugar*, which will make you eat and drink more and buy more food (isn't that the idea of the food industry?). They are hidden in many products, but nowadays it is easy to avoid them by simply reading the labels. Another thing is *reducing carbohydrates*, in particular the so called "quick sweets", bringing in too much of glucose (sugar) that cannot always be burned as fuel by the cells (lack of activity), and will be stored as fat deposits inside the arteries, around internal organs engorging them, and around the waist-line (attention ladies, this is the bulge that is so hard to get rid of). Another type of food to *reduce is fat* contained in hamburgers, sausages, hot dogs, bacon, cheeses, and creams.

It will be wise to make a *selection of proteins*, which will bring lots of energy and take a little volume, and balance it with fruit and vegetables for vitamins, minerals, and fibers, satisfying your appetite without making you swell up. It is good to take most of the sugar from fruit, it is mostly fructose and it takes a little longer to be processed, keeping your blood glucose levels steady, without the fatigue and sleepiness triggered by the ingestion of quick sweets.

Multigrain breads, lean meat, organic products, along with smaller quantities of food, should be part of anyone's choices; it is good to make a selection of the best products and reduce the amount of victuals, and consider quality instead quantity. And *give up sodas and have a glass of milk instead!*

Every person who successfully completed a well-balanced program will admit that they feel not only more beautiful, but also more energetic, and more confident, while enjoying the benefits of improving their state of health.

Sign up for classes if this can give you more motivation to stay on track, go dancing, buy new cloths, change your hair style, and don't forget to admire yourself in the mirror; this is not Narcissism, this is Gentle Therapy telling you to enjoy even a tiny victory, you deserve it!

Like anything else one desires to achieve in life, this process of healthy eating habits will require *determination and discipline;* but doing this is not only keeping our weight under control, it is exercising and improving our will and commitment.

When meditating, *start imagining how you want your body to look*, the pleasure of feeling light and slim, all the delightful moments to enjoy because you are healthier, bursting with energy and confidence, and because you triumph over a major problem in your life. *Then take this image with you wherever you go*, remind yourself of your commitment to yourself, and have this therapy at your disposal at any time and place. You may attach pictures on your mirror or refrigerator, make notes to yourself, whatever it takes, use it!

Another important point to remember is that once reaching the ideal weight for your frame and best physical appearance, one cannot live eternally on restriction. Lifetime diet is not realistic, and no one can do it. *Stick with healthy choices*, a balanced variety of good and fun foods to prepare your meals. It is good to know that it is OK to enjoy some drifting from the base line in special occasions, if an incidental indulgence does not become overindulging again. Knowing that we can, in some circumstances, forget about calories, which will help us not to fall into a real binge from too much restriction. Here again, it is important to keep a good balance and be gentle with ourselves.

Another serious problem that can endanger anyone's health is addiction: drugs and alcohol are real enemies of a good life style, and these devastating habits became serious hazards for the persons using them, as well as for the society. We all know how fast a person can fall, how repulsive their appearance and character can become. It is heartbreaking to witness the loss of family, jobs, social liberties, and the loss of dignity that can follow if addiction continues. This is even more sad, considering that it is self-inflicted and totally avoidable.

Here again, people will come with very inventive excuses, emotional promises, creating drama and hurt to their loved ones. And again, in order to restore lost health it will take serious professional intervention and total commitment from the addicted person. In addition to that, one can practice the ideas presented in this book, to help focus and stay motivated.

In order to *keep the mind diverted from the compulsive cravings*, food, drugs, cigarettes, or alcohol, one should always find different areas of interest. There are a multitude of activities that are not only enjoyable, but can keep a person involved in positive actions. For instance, there is always a good movie to watch, a library to go to where there are lots of books and conferences, social and cultural events to attend, cooking classes to learn new recipes, parks to take a stroll in, and friends and families to talk to. And there are people that can be helped by taking them to the doctor or to the stores, retirement homes where one can to do a little reading, shelters where we can volunteer some of our time. We all can be involved in activities that teach us how blessed we are, and becoming less self-centered, we are learning the bliss of giving.

In the preceding chapters we already presented some of the elements of our body's own healing natural mechanisms. It is fascinating and important to know that scientific discoveries offer more and more solutions to healing our illnesses, by using the means offered by our own physiology. In addition to cures for cancer, infections, or organ failure, there are now available treatments for more common conditions, such as arthritis and injuries. If these conditions are not always life threatening, they are definitely interfering with the ability to fully enjoy life. I am so excited to see that taking a blood sample from a patient and making a concentrated solution of platelet rich plasma (PRP), and adding to it a stem cell purified extract from a small amount of the belly fat, a preparation done in the doctor's office, can be used to treat many of these conditions. For once we all can find something good about our belly fat, since is one part of the body containing large amounts of stem cells, which makes us think that there is something good about every structure of our physic.

There is a growing application of similar treatments, and these preparations are now available in many locations, utilizing patient's natural growth hormones for their anti-inflammatory benefits, and stem cells to enhance the speed and the quality of the tissue repair. This way, we are able to treat tears of tendons and ligaments, sprained muscles, inflamed cartilages from arthritis and rheumatism, injured discs and nerves, and even injured bones. In many instances surgery is avoided, return to regular or athletic activity is fast, not to forget that there is no longer a risk of toxicity or adverse reaction to the injected graft, since the body receives back its own products.

It is practically as if we take a few cells from one part of the body, we concentrate them, and put them back to another place, telling them to do their job! I consider this manner of modern medicine as part of a more gentle therapeutic approach of medical treatments.

To further apply Gentle Therapy and enhance the benefits of any medical treatment, *we can use again the power of the words spoken and unspoken through affirmations of what we want our reality to be*. As for obtaining peace and serenity, we create the image and the feeling of the situations we want to experience, we must *create the image of the healed body, in its original perfect state*. Here again, *we must believe, feel, and truly enjoy the condition of full recovery as though already granted*.

The power of your words will create the right type and level of energy that can heal. Your words will create the contact with the higher and wiser powers of the Universe, of unlimited power and unconditional love that can heal you. And in order to help yourself, you need to know that there is a simple and universal secret: you don't have to know how, you only have to entrust and truly believe that through affirmations and prayers, what you ask for has already been granted to you.

It is why what you chose is so important; chose right, *chose goodness and happiness for you and all men, and good things will start to manifest* in your life. If you will choose a more luminous path, you have made the decision to step into a greater future.

Make the habit to replace all negativity with positive statements.
Start when you wake up, and repeat them any time:

All is good.

I am loved.

My life is perfect.

I expect only the best.

I am healed.

You may find inspiration from the Scriptures, and use these prayers for healing:

"You have given me abundant life. I receive that life through Your Word and it flows to every organ of my body bringing healing and health."

(John 10:10; 6:63)

"Heavenly Father, through Your Word You have imparted Your life to me. That life restores my body with every breath I breathe and every word I speak."

(John 6:63; Mark 11:23)

Just give yourself a chance and try; what do you have to lose?

♫

The music I chose to listen to for this chapter is **"The Requiem"** by **Giuseppe Verdi**.

Giuseppe Verdi (10 October 1813 – 27 January 1901) is mostly known as an opera composer, with many famous operas written in an Italian Romantic style. *The Requiem* could come as a surprise in the style of his compositions, since it is, by definition, a funeral Catholic Mass.

Verdi was born and lived at the end of his long life in Busetto, close to Parma and Piacenza, then part of French territory as part of the First French Empire, so he was for that time a Frenchman. Verdi was brought by his musical career to live many years in Milan and travel extensively to France as well.

Giuseppe Verdi's operas are quite popular through many famous arias including *La Traviata, Aida, Rigoletto, Macbeth, Nabucco, Ernani,* and also *La forza del Destino,* and *Don Carlos.*

The Requiem is one of my favorite musical pieces, and was performed the first time in San Marco in Milan on 22 May 1874, and it is written for vocal soloists, two choirs, and orchestra. Verdi has a unique way of treating the vocal part of the music and creating dramatic expressions of different segments of Catholic Liturgy. For instance, *Dies Irae* is repeated several times during the Latin mass, creating a dramatic contrast when the wrath of God is expressed, but *Lacrimosa, Agnus Dei* and *Libera me*, are gentle and touching.

My all time favorite still is *Ingermisco* sang by the tenor, and is one of the most moving prayers for the Lord's mercy. Please find a little moment to fill your whole spirit with this poignant segment, and imagine that you are listening to it as I did for the first time. I was in the Cathedral Saint Germain des Pres in Paris, and the special acoustic and atmosphere of the place created the feeling of one soaring with the music to the heavens.

᪣

Place to visit: **Sedona, Arizona.**

I always found that is good to combine the unique feeling experienced in a particularly inspiring place when I reflect at a problem I want to solve. I still remember the strong impression felt while visiting Sedona, in Arizona, with its places called vortexes, where a powerful energy combined with mysterious sensation of enlightenment and healing was so real, and stayed with me for a long time.

Sedona is located in northern Arizona, and in the past the Verde Valley was inhabited by Yavapai and Apache tribes, some of them still living in the region.

Nowadays, visitors are coming for the natural beauty of the area, the temperate climate, and the numerous artistic events along with a variety of outdoor activities offered year around.

There is the Jazz on the Rocks Festival, the Sedona International Film and Workshop Festival, and the Chamber Music of Sedona. There is also the Verde Valley School, an International Baccalaureate School, boarding many international students, involved in the traditional art performance.

But the main attractions of Sedona are still its vortexes. A vortex is the result of a spiral motion of air or liquid with a concentric movement toward the center of it, like a drain. It is believed that in Sedona the vortexes are not created by the rotation of the wind or the water, but by energy, such as magnetic energy. Their location is believed by many to be charged in spiritual energy, inducing the need for meditation and prayer. These places are visited and sought after for healing, as well as for the spiritual experience witnessed in these locations.

Although the person arriving in Sedona is immediately taken by its serene beauty and its subtle energy felt all around the town, there is this concentration of power emanating from the vortexes that creates this place to be so unique. The energy felt by the people visiting this place is a positive energy, inviting spiritual growth, bringing inspiration, and uplifting the soul.

If the visitor will follow the path of vortexes, he will have a different experience at each location because of the different kind of energy generated by each particular vortex. This way, one can visit the strongest energy by the *Airport Vortex* or *Airport Messa*, and marvel at the site of twisted juniper trees, where the branches followed the ascending trajectory of the energy emitted by this place, spiraling upward. This energy is The Masculine Side, since it strengthens the masculine qualities such as self-confidence, responsibility, and courage.

The *Red Crossing,* or *Cathedral Rock Vortex,* represents The Feminine Side, and although a strong energy is felt, it is a calming one, enforcing kindness, compassion, and patience.

At the *Boynton Canyon*, one will encounter the Masculine/ Feminine Balance. The vortex is located at a small knoll, and it is comparable to yin and yang association. It is very important for establishing the good balance of anyone's life, for personal growth, as well as for a good relationship with a partner.

The energy felt at *The Bell Rock Vortex* is so strong that one does not need to climb to its top to feel its power. It combines all the other types of energy, and will fill and replenish anyone with renewed forces.

The natives considered Sedona as a sacred place, and during ceremonies and meditation they pursued metaphysical experiences. Today, people search for spiritual renewal, harmony in life, and personal transformation. Healing is sought as restoration at the cell level and beyond, by resetting the vibration levels through the energy experienced. The soul is uplifted, and peace and harmony will take the place of stress and chaotic thinking.

These are the strong feelings I experienced during my visit, the same emotions other people describe when coming to Sedona. It is why I encourage anyone to benefit from its special powers and enlightenment.

"*For God so loved the world that he gave his only Son, so that everyone who believed in him may not perish but may live eternal life.*"

(John 3 – 16)

7 - LOVING THERAPY

Love, the BIG word! It is a word, a feeling we don't know where is coming from, we cannot seize it and look at it in the eyes, we cannot touch it, but it runs the world since the beginning of time. It is natural, spontaneous, and powerful, and governs overall our preferences, choices, and directions in all we do. Love is universal. Love refers not only to the person of our special interest, but is part of the way we relate with others. The selections we make regarding relations, professional orientations, social activities, eating and clothing habits, taste in décor of the home, hobbies and leisure, and so on.

Love can make one deliriously happy or destroy his life in misery.

Love is seen as the first expression of coming into this world, when a baby is welcomed with the loving look and smile of the mother. All the attention, devoted care overcoming fatigue and pain, is seen in human specie and animals as well. It is considered an instinct, be it maternal or paternal, all generated by adoring feelings toward the little delicate and vulnerable new being, but so much representing the successor of all dreams and hopes one can have.

Love is present our entire life, it follows us in what we do and feel, and it is the essence of our entire existence. It transcends the limits of our earthly life, and seems to be the common denominator of the Universal law of life and creation itself.

Love is present in every celebration as it is shared with everyone during the important events marking our lives. Nothing is more enjoyable than watching a relative or a friend radiating with happiness when getting married, receiving recognition for his achievements, being promoted, or exulting with success. Love is present when we welcome the arrival of a new baby in the family, during proud moments at graduation, engagements, birthdays, and on any occasions that are important to us. Love is present even when we lose someone, and is expressed during the funeral when eulogies and tender memories are shared remembering stories and boasting about the qualities of the departed.

Marinella F. Monk, MD

"As the Father has loved me, so I have loved you; abide in my love...that you love one another as I loved you. No one has greater love than this, to lay down one's life for one's friend."

(John 3 -16, 15 - 9, 13)

Love is the fundamental principle of Christianity and governs the faith of millions around the world for over 2000 years. Christianity is based on the sacrifice of one exceptional character, who responded to hatred and hurt by forgiving, loving, and saving humanity. Jesus continues through his teachings to spread the idea of love as the triumph over all other sentiments, and as the ultimate reason to live and die. Love is, surprisingly, and ultimately, the most powerful weapon one can ever possess.

Other religions consider love as the essential part of their spiritual values; in Buddhism and Hinduism love is viewed as a sacrament, and it is giving up selfishness, complete renunciation of oneself, taking upon oneself the suffering of the world for the love of others, without expecting anything in return.

The Jewish religion sees love in a variety of forms, from Ahava, the love of God, to grace, goodwill, kindness, compassion, and steadfast love.

The Baha'i teachings address love as "the mystery of divine relations, the spiritual fulfillment, the breath of the Holy Spirit and the manifestation of God in the world." Love is thought to be the essence of God, and His love for his creatures gives them their material existence, divine grace, and eternal life.

Ancient mythologies give real characters to impersonate love: Amor, Cupid and Venus in Roman mythology; Antheia, in Crete, Aphrodite, Apollo and Eros for the Greeks; Hathor in ancient Egypt, Ishtar in Babylonian Mythology, Inanna for the Sumerians, Rati for Indus, and Xichipilli for the Aztecs.

Other representatives of God's love are Angels, and they are present in many artifacts of ancient cultures. Romans and Greeks have beautiful winged statues or carvings in bas-reliefs; even some of the 4000-year-old Egyptian temples are adorned by angelic figures.

"The purpose of all the major religious traditions is not to construct big temples on the outside, but to create temples of goodness and compassion inside, in our hearts."

Dalai Lama

In life we experience two basic and opposite sentiments: love and hatred. Everything we do will express the choice we make as we like or dislike something or somebody. This represents the universal law of attraction or rejection, governing the position of the stars and planets, from the organization of the galaxies to the minuscule elements of the atoms. This law also influences the formation of celestial orbs, the way the landscape of our own planet is and was during its forming and transforming billion of years of its existence. This law of attraction is responsible for how our bodies, and an infinite number of other organisms, are held together.

Our feelings are an extension of this law, making all our decisions and choices a function of what we are attracted to, or turned away from. This makes us understand that love is a common denominator of universal laws, that love is the greatest power there is.

Based on this natural law, we choose our companion and close friends, the places where we live or visit, our professions, sports, and hobbies. We have food preferences, chose carefully what we wear, the car we drive, the music we listen to, and we are even peculiar about the hair style and colors we fancy. Thus, we are governed by this law of attraction at every important or minute level in every thing we do in life.

This makes us understand that if we are in harmony with our life, if we made a good balance between those two forces, one positive, love, and another negative, hatred, and if we chose more often love, we have found happiness. This means that love is present most of the time in what we do, and it becomes a welcomed friend in our life.

"Even the rich are hungry for love, for being cared for, for being wanted, for having someone to call their own."

Mother Theresa

So let LOVE be our Loving Therapy! Let us consider how through love one can reach perfection in life, shear joy and happiness, surrounded by beauty, security, and harmony.

Let's us talk about *our relation with love* itself as the first step of Loving Therapy. Do you love your life, your family, your surroundings, and your job; do you love yourself? One cannot even start considering happiness in life if he does not have a loving image of self.

Loving therapy should *start by the acceptance of who we are, and appreciation of our uniqueness.* It is *discovering and expanding our talents, enlarging our knowledge, improving our character, and growing spiritually.* Loving Therapy is arising from guilt, shame, or deprecation, through forgiveness of others and ourselves.

Once we understand that loving oneself can be the miracle cure for self-acceptance, we can move on and let this tremendous power bring us to the highest levels of personal achievement.

The basis of Loving Therapy is *filling our soul with love in every thing we think, do, or plan.* It is *replacing all negativity with the positive power of love.* It is erasing former habits and thoughts that may be dragging us down and keeping us in the dark miasma of sadness, mediocrity, and poverty. *Sitting quiet, filling our vessel with light and feelings of love*, we must erase the negative way we were relating with the world and ourselves.

One can just relax, and find peace, and when attaining a comfortable state of mind, *sort out what must change.* Then, as often as possible, one can start by replacing the negative feelings and objects of trouble, with what one desires the most. At this stage we are concentrating on obtaining the inner peace and self worth needed to further improve different aspects in our lives.

"The more you are motivated by love, the more fearless and free your actions will be."

Dalai Lama

Try to *project the best illustration of yourself*, soar to the highest, there is no limit to what you can imagine. *Focus on those reflections, carry them with you everywhere you go, let them be part of who you are about to become.* Here again, make this be your positive choice, loving the way you see yourself. Let these loving images be projected in every way you feel and act; projecting is sending out into the Universe the new version you created of yourself, which through the awesome power of love, you will make it manifest, and become your new reality.

The next step is to *contemplate with love your relationships* with people and elements of your own universe. Family, friends, colleagues, acquaintances, or anyone who gravitates around you are important, and the way you relate to them must become a loving relationship. Remember that in order to obtain a harmonious and satisfying relationship you need to make a selection. Again, you don't have to hate anyone, nor to be abrasive, or reject a person.

In order for you to have a LOVING relationship with a person, you both must be governed by kind feelings of acceptance, mutual comprehension, and respect. This is the only way one can accept the idea of a real bond, stable and lasting. Even when considering a relative, while giving a little hand in difficult times, does not mean that there is always a deep connection, and it is fine not to feel obligated to include that person into your inner circle of close friends and family. But it is very important to wish always the best even to the ones you don't feel attracted to, while trying to *surround yourself with the ones you love*.

Next, let see *what you love in life*; we are talking about profession, projects, and dreams, preferences of places to live, activities you dedicate your time to, or that you would like to include in your life. This means developing your skills, talents and aptitudes, obtaining the state of wellbeing you always desired. Your aspirations will also include success, appreciation, security, and money. Well, here is where Loving Therapy comes in, for *you must develop a LOVING relationship with every single aspect of your life.*

Knowing what you want in life, and now that you have established what makes you happy, you may start contemplating each one of the aspects of your new life. *Take time to imagine and sense that particular object or situation in vivid details, as though you already have it for real.* Feel it with all your being, love it, be thrilled and energized by that vision. The stronger you will experience that objective, the sooner it will become a reality. If you doubt, are shy in your demands, it cannot happen; it is only through absolute faith and conviction that your demands will become reality, and that you will obtain what you want.

"Choose a job you love, and you will never have to work a day in your life."

Confucius

Love is and works as a magnet: if you have a loving attitude toward your job, and you project in your mind the type of professional situation you desire as a happy and rewarding one, you will experience success. If you send love concerning your health, you will find unexpected ways to take better care of yourself, and enjoy a superior condition.

Many people think about money as a bad obsession, evil of many things in the world. This is true if one uses its power to rule and take advantage over others. If you think that money is good for you and you are not under its control, but you use money as a means to take care of your family and your needs, this is all right. If this represents the rightful retribution of your efforts and it is obtained in an honest manner, without creating any harm, this is the way to enjoy having money. The loving relationship with money must go both ways if you want the flow of prosperity to continue: *in order to receive you must also give*. Spending money when buying necessities, paying bills, or giving to charities, must be done with love, knowing that from your money other people will benefit and be able to spend. The only way for the money to come to you is if you also give, *and feel good about it.*

"Let us more and more insist on raising funds of love, of kindness, of understanding, of peace. Money will come if we seek first the Kingdom of God - the rest will be given."

Mother Theresa

You must understand that every thing you want in life must be sought with love; *loving thoughts should be your magnet to attract everything you want*: love, inner peace, success, great health, happiness, security, and wealth. You must aim high, be convinced that the Universe has infinite abilities to bring it to you. You must also know that you are not taking it from anyone, for the Universal Power is infinite and never-ending. This is good news, don't you just LOVE it?!

The whole world is in great need of love and goodness; our next step in Loving Therapy is to *become an active participant in bringing goodwill to others*, to our planet. We all are part of the energy, good or bad, that we send out as we are assisting more and more at the titanic confrontations of good and evil forces. Everyone can help the balance to lean toward a positive direction, and move forward to a world of peace, justice, and prosperity for all. Do not think that you alone cannot make a change, your power is enormous when uniting with the ones of other noble and dedicated people.

Just greeting some stranger, bidding a good day, or just offering a smile, can change somebody's mood. In a store or elevator, say something nice to another person, or inquire about their day; that can make anyone feel more relaxed and less lonely. I learned from my own experience, that when I arrive at a stop sign and another car coming from the opposite direction hurries to make it before me, I give a big smile and make a sign inviting that person to go ahead and pass first. It takes me two extra seconds to wait, and the reaction is to see a surprised, but calm and smiling face giving thanks as it passes. Holding a door a moment longer, and letting one pass ahead of you, all simple gestures of kindness that won't cost any money, can *help to make a big difference in the way we behave* in a civilized society.

And remember, when you beam a great smile with a loving look in your face at someone else, that person cannot hate you.

Considering all the violence, aggression and evil presence in the world, we can think that God must have turned His head away in disgust of men; but when He sees the grandiose power of love his beloved creatures can also display, He must forgive us in the name of Love.

Anyone can *make a habit of starting the day by sending loving thoughts to other people*: anyone who ever did something good to you or to your loved ones, people that you know or people that you never met. We all have the good fortune to know someone who has made a big impact in our life; so *you, too,* can touch somebody's life in a very special way.

Expressing love is also giving thanks, being grateful for what we have and what we receive from family, friends, strangers, and from God. Waking up in the morning and acknowledging our appreciation of all the blessings and the infinite grace we have been given, is a great joy and a happy way to start the day. We will feel even more joyful if we continue by *sending love to the entire world*, wishing all that is good to mankind. It is important to know that by doing so, we are becoming a part of this moving force and the greatest power in the Universe, the everlasting power of LOVE.

⚵

Place to visit: Venice, Italy.

Venice is a city situated in the northeast of Italy, on the Adriatic Sea, on a saltwater lagoon stretching behind the shoreline, and containing over one hundred small islands. The majority of the houses, which are built on the water, are supported by woodpiles; these piles do not decay under water because of the absence of oxygen, but they "petrify" and become as hard as stone.

The unique architecture of the city makes this place one the most beautiful in the world. Also called *The Floating City, City of the Masks, City of Bridges, Queen of the Adriatic*, or the *Serenissima*, Venice is the most romantic city to me and to many others. Venetian architecture reminds the visitor of a city out of a fairy tale book; its churches, bridges, canals, and gondolas create a one of a kind décor.

San Jacopo, on the island of Rialto, built in 421, is retained as the originating date of Venice, but statues and other artifacts from Roman and Greek antiquity have been found. For the longest, the Republic of Venice has been governed by a Doge, usually elected for lifetime. Many of them kept this Republic ahead of time, where people found refuge from the Inquisition or other religious persecutions. Venice is also the place where inventors came around the 15th century and created new printing press techniques with the invention of a paperback book concept, making books easier to print and transport, and therefore more accessible.

Because its exceptional location, Venice played a key role in trade; merchant, passenger, and warships came from East and West. Venice was an exceptional place where very different cultures exchanged products and ideas. In a more recent history of Venice, after 1100 years of Republic status, Venice was conquered by Napoleon Bonaparte in 1797, and the city became one of the most elegant and sophisticated of its time. In 1848 Venice regained its status of Republic, until 1866 when it became part of the Kingdom of Italy.

The visitor can be overwhelmed by the choices offered between cultural sites, festivals, luxury destinations, and the beautiful landscape of this city, which is an outdoor museum in itself. The archipelago containing 117 islands and 177 canals contained in this shallow lagoon is connected by over 400 bridges. Transportation is made on foot or on water, since cars are not compatible. Instead, gondolas and vaporetti (waterbuses) provide the main transportation.

A major concern regarding its particular position on the water is that the high tides are flooding the grounds and slowly the floating city is sinking. Part of this phenomenon is that six hundred years ago, in order to protect themselves from land invasions, the Venetians diverted the main rivers flooding into the lagoon and bringing the sediments filling the lagoon, which became deeper with the time. In more modern times, artesian wells were drawing water from the aquifer for the local industries; the motorized vaporetti creating vibrations were seen also as potentially destabilizing the grounds and precipitating the sinking. Some of the houses are condemning lower parts of stairs now covered by water.

The good news is that for the last decades, international efforts have been made to save Venice; as a result, it is believed that the sinking has been stopped or greatly slowed down. Although the visitor can be occasionally surprised by the Aqua Alta (high water), the inflatable gates across the seabed at the three entrances of the lagoon are to prevent the water to enter the lagoon at tides higher than 110 centimeters, and an electro mechanical system was to be completed by 2011.

The city of Venice is divided into six districts or parishes, but other close by locations are also famous including Murano Island, where the well-known glasswork has been made for over a thousand years. Nearby Burano island is known for its lace and colorful houses, while Torcello is visited for the remnants of once prosperous Roman town with its Basilica and museum.

In the past, the Jews lived confined to the Venetian Ghetto, Ghetto being the name of a foundry where the Jews lived, located in Cannaregio district. When Napoleon Bonaparte occupied Venice, he removed the gates of the Ghetto, however, the name of ghetto was retained as a definition of confinement of minorities. Lido Beach or Lido di Venezia is a luxurious destination for international celebrities, mostly in the movie industry.

Venice is very dear to me, and the first memories of this place go back to the images described by my mother when she was pregnant with me. Living at that time on the Grand Canal, while during day time my parents had some work to do fishing the ball my sister kept throwing in the water, at night my mother was cradled by the gondoliers' serenades paddling by. I believe that those peaceful and musical feelings have been imprinted in me as well, happy times that were to come back every time I returned with my husband celebrating every loving moments this place inspires.

This city has a very distinct Gothic architecture with Byzantine and Arab influences, and contains many unique monuments, such as Piazza San Marco and St. Mark's Basilica, the Doges Palace, The Clock tower built in 1499, and the Bibliotheca Marciana dating from 1547. San Mark Basilica was built in 832 in a Roman Byzantine style and topped with golden domes, boasts some exceptional features: the Greek Horses brought from Constantinople and installed on the façade of the basilica in 1254 on each side of the

Arch of Trajan. At the upper level of the façade and above the central window, the gold Winged Lion watches over the city.

The basilica is adorned at the exterior and covered inside by exceptional mosaics. The choir loft has hosted composers such as Giovanni Gabrieli and Claudio Monteverdi appointed as maestro di Capella.

If the Doges Palace with its gothic arches can be universally recognized, the Bibliotheca Marciana and its museum have been qualified by Palladio as "the most magnificent and ornate structure built since ancient times".

The L shaped Piazza contains also an elegant shopping gallery and Café Florian, where café latte was first served.

Not far from there one can stroll on the Rialto Bridge, take a gondola ride, but also attend an opera or theatrical production at the well-known La Fenice opera house.

Venice can be considered a kaleidoscope of cultural, fashion, shopping and gastronomical activities. There is the Carnival of Venice, but attractive shops offer beautiful masks and costumes all year around. One can enjoy the Venice Film Festival, Venice Biennale, museums, and private art collections such as Guggenheim's. There is a continuous display of prestigious fine arts, musical, cinematic, and other artistic events. Several *James Bond* movies such as *From Russia with Love, Casino Royal*, also movies like *Summertime, Death in Venice, A Little Romance, Doctor Who, and Vampires in Venice,* along with many video game locations, use the Venetian décor.

Venice has served as inspiration to writers and composers over time: Giacomo Casanova, Carlo Goldoni, Shakespeare (*Othello* and *The Merchant of Venice)*, Henry James (*Wings of the Dove)*, as well as Marcel Proust (*In Search of Lost Time*). Antonio Vivaldi, Andrea and Giovanni Gabrieli, Thomaso Albinoni and Claudio Monteverdi lived in Venice.

Other famous people lived in Venice, including Marco Polo, explorer from the 14th century who traveled as far as China, and Pietro Guarneri, one of the most famous luth crafters of all times. Painters were greatly inspired by Venice from the Renaissance with Giovanni Bellini, Lorenzo Lotto, Titian, and Tintoretto, to modern painters such as Vedova and Ludovico de Luigi.

♫

The music to listen to which I have chosen is **The Barcarolle** from the *Tales of Hoffmann* by **Jacques Offenbach**, where Antonia exits the scene in a gondola. The music is heard in many films like *Life is Beautiful, Titanic*, and *G.I. Blues* with Elvis Presley. As the name of the opera announces, it is a collection of four tales, all imaginary, and the *Barcarolle* takes place in Venice. This dreamy music brings special memories to me from the time I played the solo harp part on the stage of the Monte Carlo Opera, in my lifetime as musician.

The last time I heard it live was another enchanted moment; I was sitting with my husband and my daughter at an outdoor table of Café Florian on San Marco Piazza, and an orchestra from Fenice Opera was playing for summer programs. I was pleasantly surprised and flattered when the conductor asked me what I would like to hear. With no hesitation I thought that only the *Barcarolle* could express the magic of the moment; indeed, we were all elated when the music and the place recreated this perfect chemistry between the location, music, and unique memories.

Since the Barcarolle is a short piece of music, I would like to suggest another beautiful music composed by **Gustav Mahler, the *Adagietto* from Symphony No. 5**. Played in *Death in Venice* movie directed by Luchino Visconti, is the fourth movement lasting about ten minutes. It is a monumental and poignant music, and was conducted by Leonard Bernstein when played at the burial mass for Robert Kennedy in 1968 at St. Patrick's Cathedral in New York.

The *Adagietto*, a heavily emotional music, tearing apart our deepest feelings with its melancholy, is a powerful expression of romanticism. Written between 1901 and 1902, represented nevertheless a happy time in the life of Gustav Mahler, just married to Alma, the woman he loved, and expecting his first child. Herbert von Karajan, the well-known conductor, said about this music "you forget that the time has passed. A great performance of the Fifth is a transforming experience. The fantastic finale almost forces you to hold your breath." Please enjoy the music!

"The purpose of our lives is to be happy."

Dalai Lama

8 - PLAYTIME THERAPY

Having fun is another form of relaxation, without any particular need for deep contemplation or soul searching. I would relate it to play, getting inspiration from children, who don't always require much encouragement or toys to enjoy themselves. The same thing is seen in the nature, and observing small and mature animals of all kinds, we see the same need for play, and observing them we can only be absorbed in their games and have a great deal of fun.

In reality the inherent inclination to play seen in children from a very early age, but also in the offspring of any specie, is naturally inbuilt in order to learn. So they play to have fun, and they play to learn. What a better way is there to learn than having a good time?

Jaak Pansepp, a researcher in Affective Neuroscience, found out that adults, who experienced laughter and "rough-and-tumble play" in childhood, might have a lower incidence of ADHD. He suggests that this can contribute to a significantly better socialized life as adults, greater emotional resilience, and lesser tendencies to addictions.

Playing is a way to experience and experiment; this is the way one learns how to jump over an obstacle, that when making a tumble it can hurt, falling on the head or the elbow can get bruises or bleed from scratches, and if we bite someone and get bitten back, it hurts. We also find ways to reach an object that seems attractive, especially if out of grasp, curiosity helping to learn how to solve problems. All these experiences collected while playing act as stimulation to our senses, sorting out how one feels about different contacts or textures, what hurts and what feels good, and helping in the future to make selective choices.

Growing and playing continues our entire life, allowing us to accumulate more skills and knowledge. At different ages we learn different games, and not only do we need to grasp the rules of the game we want to play, but we also want to excel at it. And while we challenge ourselves, we are having fun. Otherwise why would one ride vertiginous roller coasters, jump from towers or airplanes, swim with sharks, or visit the haunted houses, if these self-defying exploits were not thrilling for the dare devil?

Babies will find quickly how to grasp and hold an object, and discover that sounds (or noises) can be produced, to their delight, when tapping on anything close by. Toys can make squeaky noises or even sing full songs, while cubes can be stacked, and wood pieces of various shapes can find their place on the motherboard. Later on, animated toys bring the world to their dimensions, and children take great pleasure activating trucks, ambulances, and trains. They discover the meaning of shapes, colors, sounds, and volumes.

But children are not aware of this elaborate process of developing reflexes, visual orientation, and appreciation of distances, or space distribution. They don't consciously apply themselves to acquire hand-eye coordination, balance, or speed; they just play and have fun. Through bumps and bruises children become aware of what can be harmful and how to avoid pain.

Pain becomes a tool that will prevent them from damage, and people that are, in rare cases, devoid of pain sensation, are very exposed to severe injuries. In some cases, children with cerebral palsy or other mental developmental conditions, that are not able to process well the sensory inputs of touch, will bite, scratch, or cut themselves in order to send to the brain signals strong enough to perceive an external stimulation. They are not "mean," nor self-destructive children trying to inflict pain to themselves, but are only finding a way to trigger a response of the cortex to a peripheral stimulation. This way, these children initiate abilities to connect with their environment.

The exercise resulting from physical play has the property to activate the production of neurotrophins, initiating the so-called brain-derived neurotrophic behavior, important in promoting neural plasticity, or ability to create new connections between neurons. Endorphins, or endogenous morphines, are endogenous opioid peptides that function as neurotransmitters, controlling amongst others, stress and pain levels. This can explain why social isolation and lack of play in children, as well as in adults, produces stress, and social isolation is frequently accompanied by chronic pain. Endurance athletes subject themselves to intense and lengthy exercise, which they tolerate because of the "high" or the "rush" felt when endorphins are released, which lessens their pain.

While children play to prepare for adult behavior, the adults continue to play for relaxation, release of tension, and for pleasure.

In the animal world we observe the same inclination to playing, in order to learn or to maintain the skills needed for survival. The juveniles try to imitate the adults, and through play improve their locomotor skills for running, chasing, and hunting. Observing their catch and release games, tag and wrestling plays that can at times be hilarious, in reality prepares them for social competition, finding food and caring for their young ones.

In the animal world, playing as rehearsing to become an adult is practically a risk-free motor training, using less energy, and serving to gain strength and techniques at a slower pace. It prepares them to carry out defense mechanisms in life-threatening situations. The juveniles use their play behavior to sample their environment and develop appropriate skills. It is believed that through play, animals in new conditions might respond in a newly adaptive way, subsequently participating to the evolution process of the specie.

The evolution of play behavior has been correlated to evolution of intelligence; birds and mammals considered as most intelligent, play a lot, but this habit is less observed in fish, reptiles and amphibians, which are considered less intelligent. The play game has also been linked to the length of time that it takes that specie to reach maturity, so the human children who have the longest juvenile period and the highest intelligence level in the animal kingdom, are observed to play quite a bit.

It is important to notice that children are inclined to enact adult roles they observe, frequently exaggerating their particularities, thus *adults exercise a great influence on the children they are in contact with and great attention should be given to that behavior.*

Looking into the developmental stages of the human brain, we will find that the brain begins to form just three weeks after conception, and by five weeks of gestation there are 100 billion neurons formed. Genetic transmission from parents is responsible of more basic information that will determine organ structures and physical features, and the way they are connected together, while the environment will determine the fine-tuning and a variety of those connections through experience. Simply speaking, the central and peripheral nervous system will be "wired" to be ready for a number of basic activities, but through the learning process, connections will be made. The more environmental stimulation – motor, sensory, cognitive, or emotional – the richer the connections formed between different areas of the brain. The cortex will be responsible for motor and sensory functions, but also for more evolved functions such as thoughts, feelings, memories, planning, and voluntary decisions.

Although the brain continues to, or rather has the ability of a life long progression, the period of childhood is critical to its development. Along with its natural growth process, the stimulation of the brain will greatly initiate changes of its structure; a newborn's brain is only 25% of the size of an adult, grows to 80% at approximately age of three and 90% by age five. The newborn brain is considerably slower (about sixteen times) than the adult's. Then the speed of neural processing increases dramatically reaching a peak by age fifteen, and slows down by age 30. The neurons having an anatomical structure that is specifically adapted to allow interconnections have small and long extensions sprouting like branches, making possible an infinity of connections, or synapses, between different neurons.

The nutrition provided to the fetus and child, as well as the health and life style of the parents, are elements influencing the size and the quality of the brain activity. An inadequate development of the brain growth from malnourishment, disease or lack of stimulation could possibly be responsible for a smaller brain, lifelong behavioral and cognitive deficits, with slower language and motor coordination, lower IQ, and poorer school performance.

This brings to serious consideration the parental and other adult influence as to how and how much the child will develop and be prepared for the future. In early life, *sound, and visual stimulation through parents' faces and words, touching and calming gestures* by holding and rocking, the baby starts to make contact with the outside world. Later on, grasping, sitting, learning how to walk, all contribute to different stepping-stones in the skills the infant achieves.

A particular role in the brain function is played by *language* learning; while the brain is wired to conduct impulses related to sound of the words, another area of the brain will have to process the meaning of the words, another area will form a response which will be carried out through the muscles forming those words as a conscious response to what was heard, and finally, another area will hear if the words spoken were correctly emitted.

Parents and teachers can greatly influence the *level achieved in mastering the language, determining the size of the vocabulary, and the knowledge acquired through readings and games*. Starting early in life to read to children will not only make them love books and develop their imagination, but will help them with school performance.

Learning an *additional language*, particularly early in life, will take advantage of the brain plasticity, or ability to use different pathways of the brain connections. The sounds of a foreign language will challenge the brain to comprehend new information, form new words and expressions as response, and use different muscles in order to form those words. From my own experience, I can say that when one speaks French uses different muscles than when speaking English.

Music is another very sophisticated manner to stimulate the brain, because when one has a pleasant time listening to music, again new connections and pathways are initiated using new brain circuits. Scientific research concluded that *classical music is beneficial by stimulating the abstract thinking*, and encourages mothers to start exposing their baby to southing classical sounds from the time the baby is in the womb.

Any activity the child is exposed to while playing, like learning to throw or kick a ball, ride a bicycle, or play the piano, *will make the neurons of various parts of the brain create new pathways*, and the practice of these activities will reinforce the circuits.

AVOIDING FALSE ENTERTAINMENT

There is an agreement in the social and psychological fields about what type of games would be most beneficial to children. In regard to video games occupying so much of our children's time, there is an overwhelming consensus that the video games have little benefit to children mental development. While video games might improve some quick reflex reactions, they do not increase intelligence. Video games will not help to build experience, nor personality, and will not expand the child's abilities to solve problems from stored information. Video games never advance children in their education, learning about science, history, or mathematics.

Educators view it as a pass time only, not helping children's imagination, nor building goals or encouraging dreams. Video games are played using reflex, uncontrolled reactions, usually aggressive before thinking or judging a situation. Not helping to develop self-control, video games are creating the risk of preparing an impulsive and aggressive society. There is also the risk of wasting too much precious free time, and wanting to escape reality and responsibilities. Very much like drugs, video games could become a dangerous habit of escaping real life.

Another danger of children's allocated time to have fun is television. There is the danger of time spend and the choices of this kind of entertainment: while television offers a vast amount of exciting programs that can educate while amusing all audiences, parents must pay attention to programs promoting mediocrity and vulgarity. Debates that are discourteous, tasteless, offensive, or rude should be blocked from children's access.

Television programs that are owned by various networks and producers, are without any doubt accountable for the content and the quality of their curriculum, and bear the responsibility of mass cultural influence. Even though their main concern is to be "popular" and have a big commercial success, the viewers consider them as representing the standards of behavior, trendy culture, and interests. In many aspects, these programs give the false impression of moral and cultural values. In reality, there are also many talented but less "flashy" artists, their life style less scandalous and creating less media sensation, which makes them less promoted by the media.

Another "having fun" time children spend is on line and on the phone. All this is part of our modern cultural changes, but again, the amount of time dedicated to those activities can become excessive and conducive to an unhealthy life style. Children and teenagers can be exposed to seriously dangerous encounters with predators met on line, and parents must take all available measures to protect their children.

SIMPLE OUTDOOR PLAY

So one would wander what to do? Well, the answer given by educators is to go back to the old free play, *stay outdoors, and enjoy more physical activities.* This will help also to prevent obesity, which has become a huge concern of the new generations.

This part of practice is described by Krista Tippet in "Speaking of Faith," discussing the biological and spiritual importance of play as "developmental sequencing of becoming a human primate. If you look at what produces learning and memory and well-being, PLAY is as fundamental as any other aspect of life, including sleep and dreams."

A prescription to simply go out and play is still the best prescription to prevent poor health and boredom.

PLAY AND LEARN

This process can continue the entire life of an adult, learning new skills, new languages, or new games. *The more we stimulate our neurons, and make them work, the more our neurons remain active, and we stay young longer.* The reason is simple to understand: if, let us say, someone wants to play the piano, having good muscles and joints of the hands and arms, good nerve control, understands that watching somebody who is playing has to move its fingers on a keyboard to make sounds, all these abilities existing, still will not allow him to schedule a concert at Carnegie Hall the week after.

Why is because that person never put all these basic functions together to work for the piano playing; we understand that one can acquire a skill only by practicing, some times for hours and years, in order to achieve that level of control. The good news is that if a disease or an accident created un impediment on performing an activity, there are ways to use this brain plasticity the children can benefit so much from, and bypass the obstacles or the injured areas by creating and using new pathways made of "wires" left untouched. It is why *is never too late to learn and to play.*

PARENTS SHOULD PLAY WITH THEIR CHILDREN

Playing and having a good time it is not only essential for adults in order to create a balanced life, but they should serve as examples to their children. We know that parents are encouraging children to spend more time in outdoor activities, but they forget to do the same, thinking that more important obligations must be given priority. Others think that their child should concentrate on more intellectual activities, and deprive their children from being children, and playing. Another category of parents are literally pushing their offspring to become champions in some sport or other competitive activity, and children are deprived from the initial interest and the scope of that particular play, spending long hours of work instead, and having no fun.

PLAY AT EVERY AGE FOR A HAPPY LIFE

One can learn that play is considered by the Greek fathers of ancient philosophy, including Aristotle, Socrates and Plato, as an important part of well-lived life. They promoted play as part of ethical virtues, along with the study of science and metaphysics. They knew that in order to live well we needed to apply a complex of rational, emotional, and social skills, and practice them in ways that are suitable to each occasion. Play was considered as important as justice, courage, honor, friendship, and pleasure. These universal thinkers understood two millennia ago the importance of play as part of society and personal well being.

There is an interesting story about Joseph Haydn and his 94th Symphony *"The Surprise."* At the end of the 18th century, Franz Joseph Haydn was a mature and very famous and respected composer. Known as the "Father of the Symphony", Haydn composed more than 100 symphonies.

While Joseph Haydn was a composer very dedicated to writing only exceptional music, he did not lose his sense of humor; the 94th Symphony was an important request for a concert during his stay in London, England, to be held at the Hanover Square Hall in 1792. The Symphony has three parts or movements, the first and last movements being played at a vivacious speed, and the middle one offering a relaxed tempo.

During the transcription of the scores for the instrumental parts that the members of the orchestra would use for the performance, the transcriptionist noticed that at the very end of the quiet second movement, marked in pianissimo, there was a last note with an indication of double forte. Suspecting an error, he went to Haydn for a correction, but the composer smiled and said, "it is not an error, it is a joke."

Indeed, during the very anticipated Premiere gala, the finest of London's society attended. As customary, after a lavish supper, an elegant audience was delighted by a lively First movement of the Symphony. When the Second movement was unfolding under the direction of the composer, the public started to relax and slowly drifted into a happy stupor. When the part came to an end, and the last few notes extinguished very quietly, suddenly the very last note struck a thundering fortissimo, and the audience woke up jumping out of the seats. Good sports, the entire concert hall soon roared with laughter. Haydn was right, he played a joke to one of most refined audiences of his time.

How can one apply Gentle Therapy after everything that has been said so far? There are two ways in my opinion: one is *cultivating a strong sense of humor*, and the other is applying *Laughter Therapy*. Along with all activities that one enjoys for fun, and all the games played, maintaining the habit of lessening the stress of a situation by looking at the humorous aspect of it, is making life so much easier and pleasant for all around. It is great to develop a routine or a tradition of finding humor in difficulties and have this practice in everyday life. We all learned from older friends sharing many years together that besides love, the most important thing was to keep their sense of humor alive and well.

Laughter Therapy is another important habit to develop in order to expand the ability to have a happy life. Doctors and other scientists have studied laughter, and many of us are aware of its physical and psychological benefits. Although humans laugh an average of 15 to 20 times a day, they belong to the only specie to know laughter. It is been said, and for good reasons, that laughter not only makes us feel good, but it is been proven to improve health and help fight disease.

Laughter is considered the best medicine, and in addition, it is infectious. It works by decreasing stress, boosting the immune system and energy levels, and even lowering pain perception. A good laugh can release muscle tension for up to 45 minutes, and stimulates the disease fighting cells and their release of antibodies, while decreasing the stress hormones, thus improving our immunity. Along with muscle relaxation, lower stress hormones released into our system improve the cardiac function and protect against heart attacks and other cardiovascular diseases. Pain levels are also lowered by the endorphin release triggered by laughter, giving a double "good-feeling" benefit to pain sufferers, having less pain and being less stressed.

Laughter plays a particular role in social interactions: people feel more relaxed, bind together, and feel happy and connected. The contagious domino effect of laughter is so important since it makes one share good times with others, feel closer and less alone under the burden of problems, and helps regain hope and strength. Laughter makes people more focused and alert, and by providing emotional release from anger or other negative feelings, brings relationships instantly closer. It is also believed that laughter improves creativity, memory, and sleep. And it works quickly by activating many areas of the brain in a fraction of a second and triggers beneficial reaction to many organs at the same time.

Many have related their stories about fighting and conquering cancer by making the habit of laughing everyday. Others become more energetic after a good laugh when the were feeling rundown, while still others believe that laughing is equivalent to a mild workout: one claimed that it took the work of ten minutes on a rowing machine to equal one minute of hearty laughing.

Laughter is free, readily available, and easy to use! And it positively changes the mood of everyone around.

I believe that in order *to maintain a good heart and, in general a good health, in addition to exercising, eating right, and not smoking, we should include Laughter in our daily therapy list.*

⚙

As a place to visit we will take a **tour of Paris, France.**

I easily could have connected Paris' visit with the Loving Therapy chapter as well, but one can have such a fun time in the City of Light anyway. Paris, the timeless city, today a city of two million people, has performed the extraordinary feat of preserving the legacy of ages while adapting to changes brought about by new times.

In the third century BC, a Celtic tribe called the Parisii, settled on the island called today *Ile de la Cite (Isle Of the City).* The river Seine was at that time larger than it is today, and surrounded the island, providing fresh water and protection. Some two hundred years later, the Parisii could not hold off the Roman invasion, and in the year 52 AD, the Roman Empire established the capital of the Gallic Province on the Isle and named it Lutetia.

This is why, when taking a stroll in Paris, one can see the remnants of two millennia of construction mixing with modern western civilization. This way, one can follow in the "Quartier Latin" (or Latin Quarter) the ancient Roman roads, and the Cluny museum dating from the fifteen century built above ancient Roman baths. Similarly, farther down on the Left Bank are the Arenes de Lutece, the Roman Arena, and they are in use even today by the Parisians playing petanque, or bocce ball game.

Over the passing centuries, the city of Paris enjoyed a steady growth of its population and a continuous cultural evolution. During the Middle Ages, Paris was already one of the greatest centers of Europe, with Gothic churches. One can visit St. Germain des Pres with its nave from the 11th century still present, or the lovely St. Julien le Pauvre built in the 12th century to attend beautiful concerts and recitals. From its square, just across a channel of the Seine River, sits Notre Dame de Paris, renown as the most beautiful church in the world. I would recommend the reading of the 14th chapter of Victor Hugo's "The Hunchback of Notre dame," and enjoy those ten pages of the description of the cathedral.

Around the 13th century the everlasting University of Sorbonne was erected, surrounded by the Latin Quarter, since the students attending the university were required to speak Latin. This always-cheerful area is as energetic as ever, with a unique mixture of bookstores, small bistros and restaurants of all nationalities, and art galleries with numerous art events taking place. By the 16th century, King Francois I created a parallel institution that would teach in French, and the College of France was born.

Close to this area one can walk to the Sainte Chapelle, go to the City Hall, or Hotel de Ville, and farther up to the Louvre, built on Roman ruins, but rebuilt also by Francois I as his palace. Today, the Louvre Museum stands as the largest museum in the world, hosting some of the most known artistic marvels of our planet, including artifacts produced by all civilizations.

Paris offers such a diversity of sites that makes it the most visited city in the world. One can find fine arts displayed in many museums and galleries, modern and baroque architecture, avant-garde buildings, and districts (arrondissements) having a distinct character. This way, visiting the old Marais, the charm is to be fund in the very dated homes and Hotels Particuliers (town homes), very much in contrast to the architecture of Montmartre and Sacre-Coeur, also old areas, dating back to 250 AD when St. Denis was beheaded there.

While inside the Marais, one can visit Centre George Pompidou with its revolutionary designs containing every expression of contemporary art; a visit to Montmartre offers a more bohemian view of a place for artists. Montmartre is topped by the majestic Roman Byzantine style basilica of Sacre-Coeur. Not far from there, the Moulin Rouge (the Red Windmill) music hall founded in 1889, entertains many visitors or regular customers. Here is where the famous dancer, La Goulue, who introduced the Can-Can, was immortalized on the canvases and posters by the very talented, but very unusual painter, the Marquis de Toulouse-Lautrec.

A few steps farther and we reach the Montmartre Cemetery containing the tombs of many famous people. One can take a walk to discover painters like Fragonard and Degas, writers such as Stendhal, Emile Zola, Alexandre Dumas, Heine, and Sasha Guitry, and musicians like Hector Berlioz and Offenbach. Montmartre Cemetery is a special place to me, since both of my parents have their final resting place there.

Paris offers so much excitement and change of décor that can accommodate everyone's taste or mood. A very beautiful stroll in the heart of the city is when leaving behind the Louvre Museum with its glass pyramid and looking toward the Champs Elysees Avenue, one can embrace a fantastic vista designed at the request of Napoleon Bonaparte, and offering miles of exceptional sequencing of monuments.

The Carousel or the small Arc de Triumph, is followed by the Tuileries Gardens, with its reflecting pools and intricate designs of flowers and shrubs, ending with two pavilions hosting the

Impressionist fine art, and arriving to the famous Place de la Concorde centered by the Egyptian Obelisk from a temple in Luxor. The promenade continues with gardens and museums such as the Grand and Petit Palais (Large and Small Palaces), then the most beautiful avenue in the world, Champs Elysees, with its restaurants and cafes, elegant stores and hotels, and the Lido, the well known cabaret.

The ascending avenue brings you the Arc de Triomphe, in the middle of the Place de l'Etoile (The Star Square), where twelve avenues are converging and were given the names of Napoleon's generals. Continuing in perfect alignment and facing the Avenue de la Grande Armee, one can take a glimpse at the far away modern neighborhood of La Defense. For the fun of it, try to watch the drivers arriving and leaving the turnabout of the square surrounding the Arch; Parisians are amazing drivers, and even though you may not wish to try the adventure yourself, you will notice that the ballet played by fast reacting cars, will manage without trouble to make it across.

Paris has such a special meaning to me and it reminds me of moments in my life, connecting these places with particular events or simply everyday's doings. Here I walk by the Conservatory of Music on rue de Madrid where I studied the harp early in my life, and there is where I attended the Medical School rue de Saints Peres, University of Medicine Lariboisiere-St.Louis, and the University Marie and Pierre Curie. There are places where I performed as a musician and practiced as a doctor. Paris is where I fell in love, met my husband in the most romantic circumstances, and married 25 years ago. Here is where I shared with my family their public successes and private moments, and is where I raised my child.

Beatrice went to school, we played in Luxembourg Park, laughed at the Guignols puppets open theatre in Tuileries, went to a number of charming children's theatres. We had our favorite places to take a walk, such as Place des Vosges and Vendome, went to Comedie Francaise, Montparnasse, Trocadero, and her favorite, the Champs de Mars, where the Eiffel Tower still one of world's main attractions of the modern times.

With friends and loved ones we went to scores of restaurants and cafes, chique boutiques, theatres and concerts in practically all concert halls and churches. We entered art galleries and stopped at the "bouquinists" on the Seine River quais to browse for rare old books. We regularly went to the local fresh markets found in each neighborhood, and marveled at the produce and other food displays, delighted by smells and colors, taking home some of the most natural and gorgeous products for a luscious dinner.

Yes, the food, in any form and savor, stylishly prepared and ready to take home and enjoy, cheeses and chocolates, tortes and pies, dairy and pates, and pastries, and breads, baguettes, croissants, all to make you feel already in heaven.

And the fashion of course, observing changes with the seasons, real catwalks on the streets and public places. My two sisters and I had our own "trouvailles" or discoveries, where we knew how to find beautiful and trendy clothing at affordable prices.

The Opera of Paris is an extraordinary place I recommend you to visit. The Opera House or Palais Garnier, the architect that designed it along with the Opera and Casino in Monte Carlo, is the largest lyric theatre in the world, and can accommodate more than 2,000 people attending a performance and 450 performers on stage.

Built in 1875 in the Napoleon III style, the Emperor who commissioned the construction, the Opera House is impressive inside and out, with the finest marbles, statuary, monumental staircases, and beautiful salons. The Hall ceiling harbors a fresco by Marc Chagall, very audacious abstract style contrasting with the very baroque interior.

The legend of the Phantom of the Opera comes from an accidental fall of a counterweight of the grand chandelier causing the death of a person, from where Gaston Leroux found his inspiration in 1910, for the Gothic novel "The Phantom of the Opera." The ghost was believed to have really existed, and the story describes a love story, where Erik, who lives in one of the underground cellars, falls in love with a singer, Christine.

Construction workers found a lake when laying the foundation, which was preserved as a tank of water, with its boat, serving for a long time as a reservoir of water in case of fire. The Opera House has seventeen levels, seven underground, some of these levels containing chorus rooms, ballets rooms, dressing rooms, set and prop rooms. There are also some of the most talented craft artists who create costumes and jewelry for the performances, and pass on their art from generation to generation. Over the years, the Opera hosted prestigious productions of lyric operas and ballets, and one can still attend an unforgettable performance.

Paris, "The Eternal City," "The City of Light," exciting, romantic, and mysterious city, has a very special place in my heart forever, and is where I always feel most at home.

♫

The music I recommend to listen to for this chapter is a collection of French music, and the selection was very difficult, since there are so many pieces of music that I like.

First is an extract from **"Carmen" by George Bizet, the "Habanera".** The action depicts Carmen, a beautiful free spirited gypsy, who lives in Seville, Spain, around 1820, and proclaims her freedom as how to live and whom to love. Her ways attract men, but also bring them trouble and tragedy. The opera in the style of 'verismo', describing the life of real people of that era, did not draw a lot of interest in the beginning, and after a few performances, tickets were given away in order to attract the public. Bizet died at 36 years of age, in 1875, and never enjoyed the enormous popularity Carmen knew later on.

The next music I recommend is **"la Mer" (The Sea) by Claude Debussy,** made of three symphonic sketches. Debussy found his inspiration during the summers spent on the French Riviera. The music suggesting the rocking of the Mediterranean waves was composed at the very beginning of the 20th century, and is a novelty in the expressionist style. It is a dreamy, dazzling music, using in the most brilliant way the diverse sounds of the symphonic orchestra. In this case as well, Debussy's music was not very well received initially, but became one of the most admired symphonic achievements over the years to come.

Another musical recommendation is **Symphonie Fantastique (Fantastic Symphony) by Hector Berlioz,** and in particular the second movement *"Un Bal," (A Ball)*. Berlioz' music is full of passion, the artist called himself afflicted with "waves of passion". The originality of Berlioz' music is that a melodic image, called leitmotiv, will appear in constant recurrence in all the five movements. *The Ball*, which introduces an exciting waltz, the main atmosphere created by the two solo harps, represents the objects of affection, sensuality, and glamour. From experience I can tell that the harp part is extremely difficult to play, and it looks like Berlioz completely disregarded the technical possibilities of the instrument, and it is why the performance of the symphony depends on the musician's and instrument's capabilities. However, this masterpiece is of such beauty that it can delight any audience.

9 - PET THERAPY

One of the greatest pleasures in life is given to us by our pets. They love us unconditionally. Their activities revolve around ours, as they follow us participating in whatever we do as they entertain us with their antics.

It is well known that people having a pet live longer, happier, and in many instances, they are more fit. There is a saying: "if you want to lose weight, get a dog."

Clinical studies show that petting an animal lowers one's blood pressure; it slows the heart and the respiratory rate, and calms anxiety. The secretion and release into the blood stream of adrenaline, the alert and defense hormone, is also slowed down. Those are objective measurements that can easily demonstrate the quasi-immediate effects of the presence of pets in our lives.

There are innumerable and touching stories about animals' devotion to their masters. How many times did we hear of a dog or a cat alerting someone of an impending danger, and how many times do their incredible instincts save precious lives?

We are riveted to the small screen when it shows a German shepherd stopping the traffic on a busy New York avenue, trying to protect her master who was lying injured in the middle of the road, trying to catch the passer-by's attention. She would not leave, risking her own life, until help was on the way; then she followed the ambulance making sure her master will be fine, and only after that she went home by herself. And all this, not to appear in the National television, but simply out of love for her "family."

Other stories talk about certain cats living in nursing homes, bringing company to the residents becoming bedridden. Oscar is a particular one, "specialized" in sensing when someone's time for passing has come, and will go to that room, and stay on the bed and keep company to that person until the end. The tabby cat brings to "his" patients a quiet comfort and reassurance that their angels will meet them on the other realm.

There are also visitor dogs, and I personally enjoyed tremendously the pet therapy visits during my weekend rounds at a Rehabilitation Hospital in Houston.

I will always remember sweet Abby, a small rescued golden retriever that I could not let out of my arms when going from room to room, and the look seen in the patient's eyes every time she was with me. I felt that she was at the same time the doctor and the healer, and her presence was better than any medication or treatment I could prescribe. I could not imagine any more Gentle Therapy!

We've seen it over and over again in the news, these sweet creatures giving simple and kind comfort to the ones suffering the most in the hospitals, to elderly, and also to young children. The seeing-eye dogs are of irreplaceable help to people afflicted with blindness, while keeping them a precious company. Dogs are also assisting people afflicted with a variety of medical conditions as service dogs.

I would like to tell you the real story of the faithful Hachiko, the Japanese dog. Hachiko, born in 1923 on a farm near the Akita Prefecture, was an Akita dog, and is remembered for his loyalty to his owner, many years after the death of them both. "Hachi" means eight, the number of the dog's birth order in the litter, and "ko" means prince. Hachiko was adopted by a professor in the agriculture department at the University of Tokyo, who lived in the suburbs of the small city of Shibuya, and took the train to work in Tokyo everyday. The professor was greeted everyday upon his return by Hachiko at the nearby Shibuya Station.

One day the professor suffered a cerebral hemorrhage and died, never returning to the train station where his friend was faithfully waiting. Although after the death of his master Hachiko was given to another owner, Hachiko escaped every day and went to look for his master, first to his old house, and after realizing that his master was not there, he went to the train station waiting for him to return. Hachiko always came precisely at the time the train was due at the station. The commuters noticed the dog waiting every day and slowly learn his story; they started giving him food and treats. And this continued for nine more years, until his death.

One student living in the area and following Hachiko's story for years, published several articles about the Akita breed dogs, and in particular about Hachiko. Soon Hachiko became a national sensation, his memory impressing the people of Japan as a spirit of family loyalty.

The Town of Shibuya gave honor to Hachiko by erecting a statue of his loving dog at the Shibuya Station in April 1934. Hachiko's remains being stuffed and mounted, were brought to be himself present at its unveiling.

During the World War II, the statue was recycled for the use of the metal, but a new one was commissioned to the son of the artist who created the first statue. The second statue was erected in 1948, and still stands even today. The station entrance near the statue is named "Hachiko-guchi," meaning "The Hachiko Exit." Each year on April 8 there is a ceremony of remembrance at Shibuya station, where hundred of dog lovers come to honor Hachiko's memory and loyalty.

When a Mercedes Benz car was ferried from one of Europe's ports to Sydney, Australia, to the great surprise of the dock custom agents upon receiving the car, a little kitty was found half dead hidden in the car. The agents took good care of the cat, which quickly became a pretty and full of energy kitty girl. When the cat was fully recovered, the employees of the Australian port ran an ad in the local newspapers for the adoption of the cat. The owner of the car in which the kitty was found, presented herself at the office, and declared that the cat already made her choice by traveling such a long trip in her car, thus the cat could only belong to the owner of the car. So the matter was easily settled. You already guessed the name given to the kitty? Mercedes.

I advocate extending our love for domesticated animals to all the animals living on this fantastic planet we live on, and to which they have the same right to share with us. One can never learn about, or admire enough the amazing variety and beauty of the creatures living with us.

Taking time to watch some documentary productions about animals in many places on Earth, experiencing their fascination by *directly observing them* close to our home, or seen during our trips, *can be one of the best therapies we provide to our souls*. This will also help us to share our love, interest, and respect for the nature with others, and should be a very rewarding time teaching our children to appreciate, enjoy, and admire all animals as well.

Since we are talking about a matter so dear to my heart, I urge all of you to react and stand up against any form of animal abuse, neglect, or cruelty. The same way we cannot tolerate to see any maltreatment against a child, elderly person, or anyone that cannot defend itself, consider that animals have little chance against stronger, bigger, or armed ones. I consider it an act of pure barbarian violence perpetrated by cowards not dignified by any civilized manners, when I am referring to people mistreating any living being, be it human or animal.

I love all animals, but it just happened that for the last twenty or so years, I have only cats, as a consequence, my husband and I, are cat lovers. Presently we have four: Pous-Pous, the oldest one, who was found by our daughter in a winter rainy day on a parking lot. Pous-Pous did not even have her eyes open, and we fed her with a dropper, the bottle being too big for her; she grew to be a beautiful calico cat and has a fixation on food: she is eighteen years old, but she finishes everyone's dish.

We adopted Princess seven years ago, when she was one year old, from the cat clinic we go to since we moved to Florida, and hoped that Princess will be a good company to the old one. Although Princess is a beautiful and sweet creature, Pous-Pous considers herself the Queen. Princess likes to talk, wants to learn how to use the computer, and became the attentive mother of the twin sisters we adopted four years ago.

Jou-Jou, (meaning toy in French, because she is very playful), and Bijou, (meaning piece of jewelry, since she is the prissy one), the two were five weeks old when we took them in, not having the heart to separate them. It was the best decision we ever made, and I would recommend to anyone to take the babies together; it is in fact a lot easier to raise them, because they play together, and learn from each other, stay cuddly and know how to share.

My cats are the best company, I never feel lonely, and they make me laugh when my spirits are down. Right now I am concentrating on writing this book, and they are with me in the room, Princess wants to help me, lying and typing on the keyboard. The others just find a comfortable pillow to take a well-deserved nap.

When I speak with my husband on the phone, they like to come close and hearing his voice, they start purring. If I catch a quiet moment and play the harp, I can't hope for a better audience, my cats are very meloman, and if I read, they are all around me giving kisses and kneading whatever they can sit on. They follow me everywhere, and if I forget to get a glass of water by my bed at night, although fallen asleep, here are the little paws fallowing me all the way down the stairs, and back up again; I call them "my stalkers!"

I was surprised by Pous-Pous in several occasions, when her reaction showed a great sensitivity; one time when my daughter Beatrice visited during her pregnancy, remember Pous-Pous used to be her cat, as soon as she arrived home and was welcomed as usual by the cat who got on her lap and started being very interested by what was inside her tummy, gently kneading, sniffing, and "looking" inside. She did that during the whole duration of her stay. Later on, when we had the visits of the baby Alexandre, who is now two, Pous-Pous will follow him everywhere, to the point that, when Alexandre had his own cat he called him "Pou-Pous"!

Recently, my husband had surgery for his eyes, and as soon as he was back from the procedure and I installed him comfortably on the couch, Pous-Pous came next to him and did not leave Robert until he was back to his usual self. One could feel her real concern, quiet compassion, and her very gentle therapeutic presence.

It is always wonderful to observe animals' behavior; they are so ingenious, and beautiful. Their wisdom and kindness can teach humans a lot about living in harmony and respect for others. We've seen in different programs on television, one of my favorites being The Planet's Funniest Animals, when animals that are considered by nature to be enemies and hunt each other, can grow to tolerate, even to love one another. We've marveled watching a cat playing with a rat, or sharing food with a canary, or when a dear runs playfully with a dog, or a swine is nursing a litter of dogs. Pets can show us that some times they are more humane than people.

A special recognition must be given to all dedicated people working in animal shelters, trying to save and find homes to animals, giving their precious time and unconditional love to lost or abandoned pets.

Our admiration is extended also to the ones involved in raising awareness of the endangered species, trying to protect and save the planet from the ravages of unnecessary destruction we inflict to animals, under the excuse that we need all the hunting and fishing to feed ourselves.

Being involved no more than a few hours a week, can be a *great therapy by taking care of an animal*, and when possible, *bringing children along to learn to love and care for our little friends*. It is such an uplifting sensation when we dedicate our time to a good cause. And being in contact with pets, and animals in general can be a wonderful way to stay aware of the marvelous nature that surrounds us everywhere.

Adopting a pet is practically always a wonderful experience for all, for the gentle therapy accompanying their loving presence, the fun, and the attention required from us to focus on a being other than ourselves. Exposing children to animals, and adopting a pet can make them *not only love them, but also teach them the responsibility of taking care of them.*

Children can be encouraged to take small jobs in the community by offering pet sitting services: it can be a pet part-time sitting service, which is a flexible, easy service that can bring some income to any student. I remember how much I appreciated having a neighbor from one of the houses across from ours coming and taking care of our pets, while bringing in the mail, and watering the flower pots. We always have been blessed with wonderful friends and neighbors who took care of our "babies", so this way we could keep them in their natural environment, and we could enjoy peace of mind during our vacations. It is surprising to see when someone takes care of your precious little friends, how much closer you can get to that person.

Pet therapy is well known when it comes to *taking children to the zoo, or parks where they can actually touch and observe closely a variety of animals. A visit to the aquarium* is also not only a walk in the wonderland, but very instructive as well.

Children and adults benefit from other activities such as *horseback riding*, either *as a physical or emotional therapy, or just enjoying a ride in the nature,* through the fields, forests, or on the beach. It is calming to discover new places while enjoying the reassuring presence of the horse.

My belief is that living in harmony with all animals is the illustration of Heaven. What more of a paradisiacal representation can there be, than people and animals keeping company and comforting each other? There are many places where people learned how to live together with animals, sharing their town with them and respecting their presence around. I enjoyed very much a place like Lake Travis, near Austin, Texas, where deer can be seen everywhere, in the streets and gardens, and their presence is tolerated with love. The locals feed the deer and slow down in their presence, and I did not hear any complaints about them, since there is no damage to the shrubs because deer have plenty of other kinds of good food to eat.

I also believe that one day we will see again all our little friends, and we will be reunited with them for eternity.

We must develop a strong sentiment of responsibility to preserve our planet and respect all creatures we share it with.

A marvelous place to visit is Hemingway's home in Key West, where Hemingway lived from 1931 to 1940, representing the most productive years of his writing. Since 1964 the house became a museum and a literary landmark in honor of the Pulitzer and Nobel Prize winning author, but the main attraction seams to be the presence of many cats, direct descendents from Hemingway's first six-toed cat. The polydactyl cats are found roaming free and well fed in the propriety, as they were during the time the writer lived there.

Built in the1850s in a Spanish-colonial style, the house located in the old town center, is an attractive and comfortable building, acquired for the sum of $8,000 in 1931 as a wedding present to his second wife, Pauline. After 1940 Hemingway traveled to Cuba, but Pauline lived there until her death in 1951. The house sits on the highest ground found in Key West, and soon after Hemingway bought the house, he built a large swimming pool, which remains one of the largest in the region. One can imagine the writer, an imposing figure, larger than life, caring tenderly for his cats, finding the quiet needed moments for his inspiration, holding his precious felines. In the garden there is even a fountain built for the cats.

No wonder Hemingway could produce *A Farewell to Arms, Death in the Afternoon, Green Hills of Africa, To Have And to Hold, For Whom the Bell Tolls*, and many of his short stories during his stay at his home in Key West!

♫

Music chosen for this chapter: **"The Animal Carnival"** by French composer **Charles-Camille Saint-Saens**. Saint-Saens, a French composer, found his inspiration while traveling in Austria, and going through a small village. Written in 1886 in the Romantic style of that period, *The Animal Carnival* is a musical suite of fourteen pieces. Starting with the *Introduction and Royal March of the Lion*, there is a succession of zoological titles, but the most known is *Le Sygne (The Swan). The Swan* is often played solo by the cello accompanied by piano or harp, and is found in one of the scenes of the film *My Summer of Love* in 2005. A famous Russian ballerina, Anna Pavlova, performed a short version of it in *The Dying Swan* ballet, more that 4000 times in the early 1900's.

The Animal Carnival is often performed in the same concert in combination with two other short musical pieces, *Peter And The Wolf* by **Prokofiev**, and *The Young Person* by **Benjamin Britten.**

In a more popular culture, various parts of *The Animal Carnival* are used in many movies, commercials, or other performances. *The Finale* is heard in *Fantasia* by Walt Disney. *The Aquarium* is played for the Space Mountain in Disneyland roller coaster, movies like *Only You, Babe, Godfather Part II, The Curious Case of Benjamin Button, The Beauty and The Beast, Days of Heaven, Visions of Light, and Impressions of France* for Epcot Center.

🚲

Special place to visit: Any Animal Sanctuary, and **Yellowstone National Park.**

The history of Yellowstone begins 11,000 years ago, when it was roamed bi Paleo-Indians who found grounds for hunting and fishing. Arrowheads, cutting tools, and weapons were found there. The name Yellowstone comes from the name of a river, first as a translation of the name given by French trappers of "Roche Jaune," changed later by American trappers to Yellow Stone.

Later on, several trappers, hunters, or expeditionists came along, starting in the early 1800's with John Colter. Yellowstone became a National Park in 1872, by the Act of Dedication signed by President Ulysses S. Grant.

Yellowstone National Park expands over two millions acres, larger than Rhode Island, and about 96 percent of its land is part of Wyoming, while three percent is located in Montana, and another one percent in Idaho.

The Continental Divide of North America, which is a topographic line running diagonally through the park, separates Pacific and Atlantic water drainage. This is the reason that Snake River flows to the Pacific Ocean, and the other rivers, although close by, but situated on the East side of the Divide, go to the Atlantic Ocean, some reaching the Gulf of Mexico.

Lakes and rivers cover 5 percent of the land, 80 percent are forests, and the remainder of the land is grassland. The average elevation is 8,000 feet, as Yellowstone Park sits on the Rocky Mountain Plateau, and its highest point is Eagle Peak, at 11,358 feet.

Yellowstone National Park boasts the largest petrified forest, where trees burned by volcanic ashes and buried millions of years ago, transformed the wood into minerals.

The Park is also the place of three very picturesque canyons, along with unique geological formations, such as the Caldera with its super volcano, and geothermal areas. The Yellowstone Caldera is the largest volcanic system in North America, and the name super volcano comes to describe the calderas formed as result of exceptionally large and explosive eruptions. Periodically the area is shaken by eruptions, the most violent one occurred 2.1 million years ago, but even a smaller one, taking place 640,000 years ago, was 1,000 times larger than the 1980 eruption of Mount St. Helens. These eruptions are part of an eruptive cycle, with climax eruptions occurring every 600,000 to 900,000 years, and some scientists predict a soon to be due catastrophic eruption in the area.

There are 10,000 geothermal features in Yellowstone, containing two-thirds of the world's geysers, including the largest active geyser in the world, Steamboat Geyser. The most famous is Old Faithful Geyser, which erupts approximately every 91 minutes, and represents one of the big natural attractions of the park.

The ecosystem of Yellowstone Park is made of 1,700 species of trees and plants, while the fauna is represented by creatures ranging from bacteria such as Thermus Aquaticus, to the mega fauna wildlife.

There are almost 60 species of mammals in the park, including grizzly bears, bison, wolves, black bears, mountain goat and lion, white-tailed deer, elk, moose, and bighorn sheep.

Besides mammals, the park is a refuge to six species of reptiles, four amphibians including the Boreal Chorus Frog, and more than 300 species of birds. One can enjoy observing the rare bald eagles or whooping cranes, and also harlequin duck, osprey, peregrine falcon, and the trumpeter swan.

The Yellowstone National Park harbors many societies protecting endangered species, with the Protective Act passed in 1873, others represented by the Animal Rights Activists, or U.S. Fish and Wildlife Services. There is a National Elk Refuge, containing the southern herd migration, which is the largest mammalian migration remaining in the U.S. outside Alaska.

Yellowstone National Park attracts at least two million visitors a year and is the most popular national park in the U.S., offering an immense variety of natural wonders. But most of all, Yellowstone brings together wildlife and humans, the best place for us to learn more about our friends, observe them in their natural habitat, and learn to respect and preserve their place on Earth.

"Art washes away from the soul the dust of my every day"

Pablo Picasso

10 – FINDING BEAUTY IN ART

Conscious artistic expression is only known in humans, and it brings the human spirit to the pinnacle of its evolution. The aesthetic sense and search for beauty in art appear to be a human phenomenon manifested by our inclination to surround ourselves with beauty, while stimulating creativity in many of us. It is in human nature to constantly look for harmony and balance, and a pleasant decorum as a place of living or natural landscaping. We are constantly adding, replacing, and changing objects, colors and ambience, in order to satisfy a disposition dominated by times and cultural influences.

Every person will make choices in everything in life, partners, locations, designing of interiors, clothes, and even a flower arrangement, based on a very personal taste, developed on preferences and styles of the time. The cannons or standards of beauty will vary and evolve quite largely with the culture, location, or period. Beauty is a matter of personal perception, although nowadays it is largely controlled by media and peer pressure.

Art and the search for beauty can change the way we look at the world, as we look to find what is providing aesthetic satisfaction. Artists can greatly influence through powerful ideas how we see reality, making us discover new and unexpected facets of our existence. Many artists marked and lasted their time by bringing originality to forms, colors and sounds, others used new materials, proportions and surfaces, making us increase our sensitivity to the way we see the world.

People are preoccupied by their physical appearance, and if this need sometimes becomes an obsession, it surely symbolizes the pursuit for beauty. Physical beauty represents the quest of a person to be attractive to others, while is drawn to someone beautiful. In many instances the value given to beauty is combined with other characteristics such as personality, grace, or intelligence.

Each civilization during different cultural periods has been represented by its own distinctive art expression, along with economical progress, social structure, and spiritual or philosophical beliefs. On many occasions, what endured the passing of time are art monuments and artifacts, that in some places still marvel the visitor with their beauty and originality produced several thousand years ago.

There is an inner urge of the human nature to manifest simple acts of daily life in an aesthetic fashion, with a strong desire of artistic creation to last for generations. Every country gives great importance to its artistic heritage and is proud of its culture.

Gentle Therapy will intervene as enhancing everyone's quest for beauty in life; *surrounding ourselves with what is beautiful in all aspects of our lives* brings Gentle Therapy to a level of sublime quality. Combining beauty and love, and finding inspiration from artistic expression brings our entire way of living to an *art of living*. And this can be done everyday and everywhere we are.

Creating a pleasant environment at home and around it will require days and years of constant search and trials, but it is a very enjoyable occupation, and many people are making it an esteemed profession. It will mean reaching out, visiting places, drawing inspiration from fine looking sites, sorting out personal preferences and developing a personal style. It will also mean bringing home these attractive ideas and converting them from art to living art. In our pursuit of beauty we will develop the desire to travel and know more about other cultures and historical changes in design and architecture.

"All suffering is caused by ignorance."

Dalai Lama

Another aspect of our artistic expression is discerning the *importance of the language* we select; literature is such a beautiful way to transmit all kinds of emotions, situations, or simply information. Reading or attending theatrical performances or poetry chapters is pleasant, entertaining, and educational. Introducing early in a child's life the desire to read is essential to open the doors of learning and is character forming. Linguistic expression is an important way to improve our verbal and intellectual capacities, and to continue to acquire additional knowledge.

We already approached the importance of having a loving manner of speaking, and now it is important to add, as part of our therapy, the importance of an elegant way of addressing others. It is part of a civilized and respectful way to address anyone, family, friends, or strangers, and ultimately it is a matter of who we are in the way we express ourselves. Without sounding "snob" or pretentious, it is important to speak in a correct grammar, and in a polite manner, and not to judge anyone by their accent. Everyone will be found to have an accent if they travel a little.

Continuing our therapy of introducing art and *beauty in our daily life*, one major aspect is the preparation of our meals. The food we love and the food we prepare with love will incorporate along with many ingredients and flavors, presentation and combination of the courses. Wine, champagne or good spring water, flower décor, fine porcelain and silverware, and seating allocation become an art.

Culinary art is appreciated by all and is associated with each country, region, or family traditions and cultural inclinations. There has always been a lot of pride displayed, and competitions are frequent between people defending their specialties or flavor preferences. This is because what and how we eat are very important everyday activities.

Artistic expression is used by all of us, as we try to reproduce images, landscapes, or faces we like. We all carry within us this secret desire to have the gift of painting, playing, or dancing with ease, and when we succeed in any modest way to bring to life our imagination, we are quite content.

A while ago, my husband and I took a few painting lessons and we had a great time learning how to bring to life on our canvas the model of our inspiration. We discovered the shaping of objects and proportions, depth and placement of colors, all the while comparing with others our pathetic limitations and mistakes. However, we discovered in my husband some hidden talents, as he made a few reproductions that received noteworthy appreciation from friends. I decided to expose two of his paintings in my office waiting room, and many of my patients inquired about the artist. They sincerely admired his talent, since they did not know the origin of the artwork.

All this is to say that it is so important to *dare to try and express whatever gifts* we all have within, and the satisfaction will be considerable.

Dance is another form of expressing beauty in art. Dance enables us to enact through the movements of our body what we feel inside. The way we hold our head, the motion of the hands and legs, along with the rhythm we follow to harmonize our steps with the music, will bring our whole being into a different level of vibrations. In many cultures, people will let their mind and body join a frenetic intensity of speed and sounds bringing them to a true trance. They consider these ritual dances as a magical release of a number of tense situations.

Music and dance have been described, depicted, or engraved in stone, in all times and all cultures, as symbols of formal ceremonies or joyful celebrations. Dancing of joy, for fun, or as an art exercise, is part of our society, and represents a spontaneous need to let our body release energy and express our emotions.

There is a more structured form of therapeutic dance through Dance Movement Therapy (DMT), used by professional therapists in addressing some psychological, cognitive, physical, behavioral, and social conditions. Sessions of dance therapy are offered in health facilities such as rehabilitation centers for medical and mental disabilities, nursing homes, or day care facilities.

Applying the principle that body and mind are inseparable, movements of the body will influence the way we feel. One can learn from the non-verbal expression of dancing, how to improvise, and let a spontaneous whim come free.

We all benefit from the wonderfully therapeutic effects of dancing, by improving our balance, coordination, and our psychological well being, as well as releasing stress and gaining a sense of rejuvenation. Dance is the best cardio-pulmonary conditioning; it is having a good time, without even knowing that you are actually exercising and expressing some hidden artistic talents.

The therapeutic benefits of music will be presented in one of the chapters to follow. *So, go out and have fun, dance, sing, paint, decorate, and unleash your own creativity* for the thrill of blissful times to enjoy.

🚲

The place we will visit this time is **Florence, Italy.**

Florence is the epitome of art and beauty, and although considered as the birthplace of the Renaissance witnessed between the 14th and 16th centuries, its existence can be traced back to prehistoric times. Florence appears to be the lieu of uninterrupted cultural changes and evolutions.

Some remains were found from an Etruscan village dating back to the Iron Age. The old Roman site of the town conserves even today its originally designed network of streets. About year 59 B.C. the city was laid down on the Florentine basin at the confluence of the Arno and Mugnone rivers, where an army camp was built for veteran soldiers at the request of Julius Caesar as a stronghold of the area.

A city named Fiorentia developed rapidly thanks to its favorable position, and trade and commerce grew and thrived during the early Christian era. In antiquity, Florence was protected by thirty-five towers dating from the Roman presence, two of them are still standing in the city center; the towers were built initially for defense, but by 13th century they were occupied as houses.

Churches like San Lorenzo and Santa Felicita were built in Florence as early as the 4th century. Eventually Florence saw changes with the presence of successive periods of turbulent rule by the Ostrogoths, followed by the Byzantine and the Lombard presence.

In the 8th century Charlemagne conquered Florence, which became part of the Duchy of Tuscany. Florence continued to grow, and enjoyed a Golden Age by the second millennium, building basilicas in the Romanesque style, like Santa Trinita and Santa Maria Maggiore. This prosperous age continued with the arrival of the Medici family during the mid-1300's. The Medici were essentially bankers, although they were greatly supporting arts and were instrumental in the Renaissance explosion.

During this period, money was reinvented in the form of the "Golden Florin," a term invented by Petrarch, helping to bring Europe out from the "Dark Ages". With the arrival and domination of the Medici, the town was able to finance a large part of Europe, from Britain to the Eastern confines of the Danube, including the Vatican, and boost the industrial economy of that time.

Taking a little detour to consider the historical impact of the Medici family, not only in Florence, but also in Europe's history, we find ramifications extending through the 20th century. By the early 15th century, the Medici family took control over the life of the city, although Florence still claimed a democratic status. Noble, powerful, rich, and on occasions ruthless and brutal, the Medici nevertheless played an essential role in the history of Florence as patrons of the arts, and financial and cultural developers of the city.

The first Medici to impose control over Florence was Cosimo. Lorenzo was one of his grandsons, and he was the one who started to commission artwork by Michelangelo, Leonardo da Vinci, Botticelli, and Raphael. Later on, the extraordinary art collections of the Medici family were displayed in the world renowned Uffizi Gallery founded in 1581 by Francesco I de Medici. This gallery is connected through Vasari's elevated corridor inside the famous Ponte Vecchio, to the Medici residence, Palazzo Pitti.

These places contain some of the world's marvels, where drawings, paintings and sculptures by the artists already named above, and also by Verrocchio, Filippo Lippi, Correggio, Veronese, Tintoretto and Caravaggio, along with Flemish artists such as Rubens and Rembrandt. The visitor will be in awe in front of large rooms filled with the best selections of antique Roman and Greek sculptures, exquisite frescoes and tapestries. The Uffizi gallery hosts the "Birth of Venus" and "Primavera" by Botticelli, Michelangelo's "Holy Family," and Raphael's "Madonna of the Goldfinch."

Another famous member of the Medici family was Catherine de Medici (1519 -1589), who married Henri II king of France. Her children included three kings of France, (Francis II, Charles IX and Henry III), and she ruled France herself as regent until Francis had attained the adult age. She is directly related to Henry IV, Elisabeth of Hapsburg, Phillip II of Spain, and queen Mary of Scots. Catherine was the one to bring Renaissance to France, and she greatly participated in building some of the famous castles of the Loire Valley, in particular when Leonardo da Vinci came to the area. Leonardo da Vinci worked also for Louis

XII and Francois I, participating in the construction of castles of Amboise and Chambord.

San Lorenzo basilica, named after the Lorenzo IL Magnifico, contains the Medici Chapel, where most of the family members are buried according to the traditions of prominent families of that time.

The historic center of Florence, declared a World Heritage Site by UNESCO, attracts millions every year. Florence is one of most beautiful cities in the world, offering a large diversity of the best cultural displays. Art is represented as architecture, fine arts of all kind, music, literature, philosophy, even cuisine and fashion. Art is present everywhere in Florence, in its squares, museums, churches, parks, and gardens.

Architectural treasures can be admired just by walking the streets of Florence; the visitor can wander in the Piazza della Signoria with its statues by Donatello and Cellini, along with a copy of David by Michelangelo, the original been exposed at the Academia dell'Arte. One can admire basilicas like Santa Croce, where the tombs of Michelangelo, Dante, Machiavelli, and Galileo are located. Santa Maria Novella, San Lorenzo, and the Tempio Maggiore are other basilicas to be admired.

The most representative of the Renaissance architecture is considered the Duomo or Santa Maria del Fiore, built in the 13th century, designed by Brunelleschi, and dominates the city with its domes and towers. Close by we also find the beautiful towers of Campanile, designed by Giotto, and the Baptistery. In the same period, as a symbol of the wealth and power of the city, many palaces were erected, including Palazzo della Signoria, where one can admire the Neptune Fountain and the equestrian statue of Cosimo I de Medici. Palazzo Vecchio, for a long time residence of the grand duke Cosimo I, now is a museum containing splendid collections of art.

Palazzo Davanzati, containing the Museum of the Florentine House, Palazzo del Bargello, and the Accademia, host unique artwork by Michelangelo, Donatello, and others.

Arno River is crossed by the famous Ponte Vecchio, which dates from the Etruscan period, and was rebuilt in the 14th century. Along the bridge, the passer-by is tempted with articles sold in the shops lining the Ponte, particularly jewels of gold. On the opposite side of the river one can visit the large Palazzo Pitti, with the private art collection of the Medici, or go for a stroll on the adjacent Boboli Gardens.

Other famous names associated with Florence are Boccaccio, Niccolo Machiavelli, Franco Zeffirelli, Ferragamo, and Roberto Cavalli.

Florence is a place to visit and enjoy the enormous cultural treasures present at every corner, a place to return to and absorb even more of its beauty and traditions, and takes it within for the dreaming time about what beauty and art can bring in our lives.

♫

Music to listen to: **Antonio Vivaldi, "The Four Seasons."**

Vivaldi composed the *"Four Seasons"* in 1723, as a set of four violin concertos, and is one of the most known pieces of Baroque music. First concerto is *"The Spring"* ("La Primavera"), naturally followed by *"Summer"* (L'Estate"), *"L'Autunno"* (Autumn"), and "*L'Inverno*" (Winter). It is believed that Vivaldi himself wrote four Sonnets, each one representing one of the seasons, and having sections of three parts accompanying the three movements of each concerto.

Vivaldi, who was born and lived most of his life in Venice, was mainly an opera composer, but as a violin player and teacher, wrote many concertos as practice exercises for some of his most talented students. However, those concertos became very successful in many countries of Europe, some played at the Luis XV royal court.

It is less known that Vivaldi became a priest, even though it was against his own will, but he wanted to help his deprived family, while he could obtain free education. Although Vivaldi remained a priest his entire life, he did not practice as a clergyman, but he continued to be part of the Holy Church as a musician. He was appointed to the very prestigious position of choirmaster of St. Mark Basilica in Venice, and in charge of the musical performances of religious services, which included music for organ, choir, or orchestra. Among his other duties, Vivaldi was to teach music and direct the orchestra of very talented young orphans living and getting education at the Ospedale della Pieta. This orphanage is located close to the St. Mark Square, and can be seen even today.

Vivaldi was commissioned to write for a number of official and private events, and his extraordinary ability to compose exceptional pieces at a record speed remained legendary. For the Hospedale della Pieta, only, he would write one concerto every two weeks, or a cantata per week. Vivaldi produced also melodies for organ, solo voices, and dramatic large ensembles of choir and orchestra.

Vivaldi's personality remained legendary for his handsome features, and his passionate and fiery character. He is loved by many for his contribution to expanding the instrumental techniques to previously unknown heights, for enriching the Italian musical style, and for the beauty of his exquisite music.

11 - OUR HOBBIES

Relaxing, or performing favorite activities in and around the house, or discovering and directly experiencing different places, are activities not only enjoyable, but also necessary for a balanced and fulfilled life.

This chapter, addressing our hobbies, is in truth about challenging ourselves. I think that Gentle Therapy covering different aspects *of our life should include the idea of going beyond our limits*, reaching farther and higher than our usual cocoon. Just taking a vacation and visiting unusual and attractive places can be a welcome break from our daily routine.

In many instances we need a little push to complete the arrangements needed at work and other social or familial obligations, and overcome the guilt of straying away from our responsibilities. This is also part of the challenge, but being gentle with ourselves means also learning how to be generous by allowing more free time for ourselves. Finding time to be a child again, or to fulfill a life long dream, is not only OK, it is therapeutic.

I am writing about these kinds of activities because I recommend that everyone *takes the time to complete a special project dear to their heart*, even if it can only be done rarely, to *break the routine and immerse into a different world and new pursuits*. It is refreshing for the body and the spirit, as well as for the relationships, and gives to all a welcome boost to go back to the daily routine at home.

It is good to start, if not already done, with *a wish list of places or things we want to accomplish during our life*, in contrast with our regular routine. That can be climbing a high mountain, air gliding off a cliff, or jumping out of a plane in a parachute. It can be skiing down the glaciers of the Alps in the summertime, or it can be taking a helicopter ride over a volcano or through a canyon.

In order to *expand our vision of the world*, we must leave behind the limitations we imposed on ourselves when we created our comfort zone. We will benefit from embracing what our planet offers us in its entirety, with its splendor and amazing diversity.

In order to live happier, we must all learn about each other, understand each other's cultural and religious background, and ways of living, including art and cuisine. The biggest challenge here is to open our hearts and minds, and accept other habits and philosophies of life, and realize that when we understand different people's behavior, we all get along just fine. From there we can embrace the idea of a peaceful world, and respect the beauty of the natural life on our planet.

"When I see Your heavens, the work of Your fingers, the moon and stars that You set in place, what are humans that You are mindful of them, mere mortals that You care for Them? Yet you made them little less than a god, crowned them with glory and honor. You have given them rule over the work of Your hands, put all things at their feet. O Lord, Our Lord, how awesome is Your name through all the Earth."

(Psalms 8:4-7, 10 (New American Bible)

I had the pleasure to write some pages of this chapter finding inspiration during my second trip to Hawaii, during some quiet times by the window or the balcony of my cabin, during our sailing time to the islands, a restful time I was longing so much for. My intention is to take my reader, my friend, with me and enjoy together this new adventure, sharing the places and feelings of this enchanting voyage.

Hawaii is a great place to go for a visit or for a grand challenge; there is something for everyone, from beautiful sites, flora and fauna, artwork, music and dance, to beautiful people and their cultural richness. It leaves one with the desire to come back again and marvel even more. Because of the geological singularity of Hawaii as the most isolated archipelago in the world, 2500 miles away from the closest firm land, over 90% of its flora and fauna are found nowhere else on the planet. It is why the visitor in quest of a unique experience should definitely consider coming to Hawaii. It is good to mention that, although Hawaii is a big touristic attraction, there are many under populated areas, because of the particular geography of the islands, some places are inaccessible directly from the land.

To make things even more attractive, the lovely scenery, turquoise waters, and the tropical climate, would delight the most demanding visitor.

Hawaii has eight major islands, with some 96 small offshore islands. Hawaii is smaller than Fiji and slightly larger than Connecticut.

About 25 million years ago, the islands were formed coming out from the bottom of the Pacific through spectacular eruptions of underwater volcanoes. They are relatively recent islands, the Big Island is the most recent and also the biggest, and active volcanoes are part of the natural life of the Hawaiian Islands. Kilauea and Mauna Loa, in Hilo, are the most active volcanoes in the world, while Haleakala is the largest dormant volcano. The Big Island has mountains that are high enough to be covered with snow. Mauna Kea with its 13,796 feet above sea level is considered the highest mountain in the world if we measure its elevation from the bottom of the ocean, with 33,476 feet, by far dwarfing the Himalayans.

The first inhabitants were present in the islands, coming from the Marquesas and Tahiti around 1200 AD. Then followed the Vikings, Christopher Columbus, and in 1778, Captain James Cook. It became a kingdom under the Big Island's Chief Kamehameha, who united with the other islands by 1810. Later on, Hawaii found great interest from the British, French, and northern American states during the Civil War. It is interesting to note that the northern United States were getting fresh produce and sugar from the southern states, until the supply was interrupted by the Civil War. The northern states soon found an exceptional favorable climate in Hawaii to grow new plantations of sugar.

Initially welcomed to the islands, soon the new Yankee plantation owners had the control of 85% of production. This played the final role in the pressures exercised on the isolated Queen Lili'uokalani to sign in 1893 the agreement for the United States to take over Hawaii. At that time, military units were stationed at O'ahu, or Oahu, at the location now known as Pearl Harbor, already in place for the safety of the sugar plantations and their crop transportation to the continent. In 1959 Hawaii became officially the 50th State.

The breathtaking natural beauty of the islands offers lush tropical vegetation, strange lava runs, high mountainous peaks and vertiginous cliffs of hundreds of feet dropping directly into the ocean, at times carrying lava rivulets with them. Waterfalls and canyons are impressive and dramatic, and are not far from shell white or black lava beaches, ready to welcome the visitor.

One can wonder at the spectacular view of the canyons, or enjoy the prowess of surfing high raging waves. Hawaii is definitely the ultimate place that offers very contrasting experiences, and for the more adventurous ones, it is the place for unique moments. From the helicopter rides above canyons and volcanoes, waterfalls and unexplored beaches isolated by walls of vertical cliffs, to a spiritual experience of Hawaiian rituals still in practice, a person can live very special moments never to forget.

🚲

The Big Island is not only the biggest, nearly twice as the size of all the other islands combined, but is also the youngest. It continues to grow, thanks to the volcanic activity of Kilauea, and since 1983, has added 300 acres of coastal land. There are two distinct geographical divisions of the Big Island: a lush and rainy east coast tropical side, and a dry and sunny west side. Because of this disposition, The Big Island offers a great variety of landscapes, contrasting from lush coastal valleys or rain forests, to desolate lava flows, rugged sea cliffs, deep canyons, and deserts. One can see the scenery changing from rich sugar plantations and cattle ranches, to the huge steaming caldera of Mauna Loa, and marvel at the site of fairytale waterfalls.

In addition of the two big towns Hilo and Kona, The Big Island has smaller inviting towns, untouched by tourism, with a slower pace of activities, where more adventurous people will see wild horses, fishing villages and farms, and where locals are still living from the land. Adventure can be found also in surfing near the coasts of Kona or Hilo, wind surfing or diving, snorkeling or whale watching. You might want to catch a 1000-pound marlin on a deep sea fishing trip, do some hiking and enjoy the superb vistas, go horse back riding on the beach, golf, or even ski in winter time. But one of my favorites is a helicopter flight to truly enjoy most of the unique and splendid sites of this wonderland.

Because we are talking about challenge, the helicopter ride we took in Hilo was an unforgettable experience. It was during the trip my husband and I took in Spring 2011, to celebrate our

25th wedding anniversary. Flying in a helicopter over Hilo was mostly about discovering the volcanoes from above. Our young and experienced pilot introduced us to the latest landscape transformations made by recent eruptions.

The view from above is so unique that one should definitely make it as a desirable project. The lava runs cover a very large part of the center and western side of the Big Island, and a continuous chain of volcanic activity can change over a few hours. Gazing at the lava spewing in the caldera of Mauna Loa and Kilauea, watching the steaming sulfurous gases escaping from Pu'u O'o, and flying over miles of psychedelic visions of the tortuous lava fields, covering villages and blocking roads going nowhere, gives the feeling of being on a different planet.

And to continue the unexpected, in the middle of a lava field, remains a single surviving house untouched by the lava flow surrounded by its quarter of an acre of tropical vegetation. The owner of the house chose to stay and live there, completely isolated, but receives visitors flown in by helicopter for a bed and breakfast experience. The desolate landscape vision is contrasting rapidly when approaching the beautiful water falls of Akaka, with its 422 feet of tinsel flows. On the Big Island one can also admire the lava tube tunnels while going to the lush Nani Mau tropical gardens, or visit the Rainbow Falls in the rain forest.

🚲

Oahu is the most developed of the Hawaiian Islands, and contains approximately 75% of the Hawaiian population. Commonly known places are Pearl Harbor, Waikiki, and Sunset Beach; less expected is to find the only royal palace in the USA. There is something for everyone to enjoy, and Oahu is the most affordable island in Hawaii. There are many beaches and parks, but based on the coastal position, they have peculiar climate and water conditions; so when the waves can be rough on one side, one can find calm waters on the other side. The beaches can be made of white sand as in Waikiki, and Oahu can also offer the world renown 20-30 feet waves for surfers to ride on the North Shores all year around at the popular Makaha Beach, or many other spectacular sites.

As on the other islands, snorkeling, hiking, golfing, fishing, scuba diving, horseback riding, and also helicopter or glider rides, along with many botanical gardens visits, are available. The visitor should stop at the very emotional Pearl Harbor memorial site. This is a part of American history still vivid in the events linked to World War II, and it includes a museum and an offshore memorial at the sunken USS Arizona. It commemorates the 7 December 1941 attack by 350 Japanese planes, that killed 2335 US soldiers and sank more than 20 ships, and destroyed 188 airplanes in less than 2 and a half hours.

The average age of the men on the Arizona was 19, and the 1177 of them who lost their lives are left in the sunken ship, remaining entombed in its hull and buried at sea. The battle ship lays 8 feet below the water, and still oozes one or two gallons of oil a day. There is a very touching feeling about this place, and one is deeply moved by the lingering sentiment of the ones that made the ultimate sacrifice in this paradise-like place, sincerely wishing that they found the eternal one.

The challenge here was going on the submarine Atlantis and reaching without any difficulty more than 115 feet below the surface. While waiting on the boat that brought us offshore, and searching for the submarine to emerge breaking the surface somewhere, we were delighted by the show the humpback whales put on for us.

Going under the water, there is nothing to compare with looking through the windows at the unexpected and enchanting spectacle unfolding in this element that is the most prominent on our planet; it is full of life and a large variety of species, busy with their own activities, but so curious to look at these strangers adventuring to their territory. The décor changes continuously, more exciting and fascinating, from coral formations with its myriads of fish and miniscule crabs living there rent free, sharks roaming in the wreckages of an airplane or military sunken vessels, tropical fishes of all shapes and colors, sponges, scores of sea urchins and shells. Going under the surface reminded us quickly about the extraordinary existence of an exhilarating, but less known world.

The good fortune here is that being in the air conditioned, fully pressurized comfort of the submarine, would cut through weeks or years of training on scuba diving, to allow anyone to descend to an impressive depth, not to mention that the sub will cover a large distance offering many more sites to visit, and makes one feel like a guest of Jacques Cousteau's team!

🚲

From there, jumping to **Kauai**, another of the eight main islands, the scenery changes again. Known also as *"The Garden Island"* or *"The Eden Island,"* the nature is sovereign in Kauai. King Kamehameha has never conquered this island, but Kauai voluntarily joined the alliance with the other islands. It is believed that the Spanish explorer Gaetan, was the first to reach this island in the mld 1500s, before captain Cook in 1778. There is a legend about the race of little people, called menehunes, living a happy life in the island as elves, and building great structures and artwork in stone.

Around the year 1000 when the first Tahitians came to the Island, they made the menehunes build temples, complicated irrigation networks, and other fine stone works; while some of these artifacts remain from the menehunes, the Tahitians created the legend of the little happy people.

Tahitians, arriving in a second wave in the 1200's with a fleet of double-hulled canoes, introduced to Kauai sweet potatoes and taro, from which is made the local popular Pui. If you are not a native of Hawaii, you will probably never get used to like Pui, a glue-like texture after taro is cooked and smashed, but the locals use it as "filler" for many other dishes. The Tahitians introduced also sharkskin drum made from Pahu Hula, a shark fished in Hawaiian waters as well, and serving in manufacturing the drum used for hula dance even today.

In the center of Kauai can be seen Mount Walaleale, the long extinct volcano that gave birth to the island, and representing the wettest place on earth, with 450 inches of rain yearly. Centrally located as well is Waimea Canyon, desert-like and grandiose, but the name meaning strangely red (Wai) and fresh water (mea), where NASA trains some of its astronauts. The Na Pali cliffs ranging over 14 miles of steep walls on the Northeast coast can be approached by boat only. This was the place of ancient rituals where the tribal chiefs were buried, along with their sacrificed companions.

Another attraction of this island is the tropical sanctuary of Fern Grotto, a natural amphitheater creating the settings of one of the most romantic places on Earth, becoming the Capital of the Honeymooners in the world. Indeed, this splendid place is where many come to tie their lives together, while the Hawaiian Wedding Song is performed by the local chorus. Robert, my husband, and I visited the Fern Grotto and enjoyed a mutual recommitment falling under the charm of the traditional love song.

The island of Kauai has another particularity; with chickens running free everywhere, since the mongoose, their predator, was destroyed because they were eating the eggs of the ground-nesting birds. They are cutting through the traffic crossing the roads with their chicks behind, and one can have an organic grown meal out of a chicken, if he can catch one.

Attending a luau and feasting on a Hawaiian meal is another must-do experience. We had the joy to attend one during a typical ceremony, with the wild hog being taken out from the pit after roasting slowly on the palm leaves. All this was taking place in a botanical garden; I would call it Eden Garden for its splendid beauty and serenity, where peacocks were gently parading everywhere.

Trees and flower bushes with vibrant colors, ponds, bridges over small streams and water fountains, all created a perfect image of an idyllic world. Fish and birds were coming close and looking at me in a friendly way, making me suddenly feel transported into another dimension where communication became so easy. I had the absolute conviction that we understood each other, that there was infinite kindness and love in the way they looked strait into my eyes. That was one of those mystical moments we all want to know in our lives, as a challenging Gentle Therapy experience.

As we followed inside for the luau, served in an open pavilion, our hosts adorned us with fragrant leis made of purple orchids. Hawaiian music and dances continued during the gourmet lunch served by the kindest people imaginable. The ladies were all smiling and dancing gracefully, wishing us to come back, which we certainly will.

Other thrilling images to enjoy while in Hawaii are watching the playful whales; they can be seen close to any island, although certain spots are indicated as "guaranteed." The whales come to spend the winter months in Hawaii, breed, and have their calves, then go back to Alaska for summer. The humpback whales are fortunately coast-huggers, and they can easily be observed from the shore. They have been hunted almost to extinction until 1966, although their slaughter continues illegally in some places on the planet.

Some 1,000 humpback whales arrive in Hawaii in November and enjoy the warm waters until the end of April, under the close protection of the Marine Mammal Protection Act and the Endangered Species Act. It really is a great joy to see these large and gentle giants of the seas teaching their babies or jumping with their young ones.

Kauai offers stream-fed lush valleys, geysers like the Spouting Horn, and magnificent beaches. A famous beach is Lumahai, considered the most photographed beach in the world, seen in movies like *"South Pacific"* and *"Raiders of the Lost Arc."* The Honopu Valley on the Napali Coast was the jungle home for *"King Kong"*, but also the *"Jurassic Park"* and *"Avatar"* real ground settings.

🚲

Maui was one of the longtime expected destinations, and will remain as one we will always want to come back to again. A quick geographical look at the island tells us that Maui is the second largest of the Hawaiian Islands. Maui is formed by two massive volcanoes that enclose a beautiful tropical valley between them. The valley is lined with picturesque waterfalls of Hana, along with pineapple and sugarcane fields.

A major attraction of the island is Haleakala Crater, the world's largest inactive volcano, at 10,032 feet above the sea level, towering at the Center of Haleakala National Park, with its 3,000 feet deep, seven miles long, and two miles wide crater. Haleakala means "House of the Sun," since the massive depths of the crater hold both, spectacular sunrises and sunsets. Mark Twain wrote after watching the sunrise at Haleakala: "It was the sublimest spectacle I ever witnessed."

Maui has over 80 swimmable beaches, more than any other island, and one can choose from the rainbow the color of the beach, ranging from white, gold, green, garnet, and black sand. From there, one can admire, close to the coast, the playing of the humpback whales, where they come more numerous than in any other part of the world.

Above all, Maui will forever be a very special place for us, engraved in our memory for our marriage vows renewal celebrated on the beach, framed by one of the most spectacular views in the world. On a clear April sunny vibrant day, a Hawaiian minister celebrated in a simple ceremony, the traditional wedding vows renewal, where the island spirits were invited to wish to Robert and I, a long, happy life together.

These magic moments gave us the impression that we were in a timeless place, that we just got married, and a universal God was blessing our union for an eternal bliss. After the ceremony, Lisa, our guide, a beautiful and very nice young lady, made some designs on the sand with hearts made of orchid leis. Next to a heart shaped black lava stone I found under my bare feet right at the place where we were standing, she wrote "Just Mauid," describing exactly our feelings.

♫

Music to listen to I recommend this time is **Franz Shubert's "Unfinished Symphony."**

Like the title of this Symphony, I consider the flow of life, and the very special connections with people and places, to never end.

Although started in 1822, the symphony was never completed, and is the Symphony No 7 in the order of his compositions. The first two movements were finished, but in the classical tradition and the style of the composer, two more movements were to be expected. Shubert left however a scherzo for piano along with two pages orchestrated. It has been also suspected that the fourth movement was somehow detoured from its initial position, and that Shubert used it instead as the "Entr'acte" in B minor for the play *Rosamunde.*

There has been extensive debate about the fate of the music left behind by Shubert, and there are some indications suggesting that the piano score was intended to be the Third movement and the incidental music for *Rosamunde* as the Fourth movement. They are written in the right tonality (B minor) and orchestral instrumentation of the two initial movements have a similar lyrical mood.

Shubert handed the written Symphony score in 1822, to Anselm Huttenbrenner, then in charge of the Graz Music Society, who granted Shubert an honorary diploma in 1823.

It has been speculated that Huttenbrenner received the manuscript completed and delayed its performance, since Shubert lived until 1828 and could have had the time to complete the music, if not already done in 1822. Some scholars make reference to pages torn out after the two pages of the scherzo, and they are not in agreement if the damage was permanent. What it is known is that Huttenbrenner waited until 1865, 37 years after Shubert died, to reveal the existence of the last Symphony left by the composer.

In 1928 at the 100 years Anniversary of Shubert's death, Columbia Gramophone launched a large competition for the completion of the Unfinished Symphony, and close to 100 were presented. Some have been performed, but even the winner of the competition, Frank Merrick, has been long forgotten.

Nowadays, the Unfinished Symphony is performed including the piano score of the *Scherzo* as the Third movement, and the *Entr'acte to Rosamunde* as the Fourth movement, or is presented only by the first two movements.

During his short life, Franz Shubert lived only 31 years, the composer was consumed by the need to compose music; he left an extensive art work including songs (lieder), symphonies, chamber music, and operas. Franz Peter Shubert was born in a small suburb of Vienna in 1797, to a schoolmaster and a mother who was a former cook.

The family had an inclination for music, performing chamber music on Sundays and holidays, and the father initiated the young Franz to violin. Although exposed to a decent education, in these times one could not expect to subside from performing art, Shubert struggle with material scarcity his entire life. However, the young Shubert greatly benefited from being admitted to a boarding school in Vienna from the influence received from Antonio Sallieri. Sallieri recognized the young Franz' talent and encouraged him, as the young Shubert started to compose.

Shubert lived practically helped by friends, some offering access to their homes, even at the end of his life organizing musical parties called the *Shubertiaden*. Some philanthropic help was offered for the three ceremonial cantatas, and two of his symphonies (No 4 "The Tragic Symphony", and No 5.) But overall, Shubert remained penniless for the daily needs, and was largely dependent on a group of friends who provided him with meals, and even paper for his writing.

Usually his day will start early in the morning and Shubert will begin right the way to compose well into the day; he would have a meal paid by his friends around 2 pm, and will go back to write some more. His power of concentration and his inspiration were phenomenal, and he was able to compose 5 or 6 songs during the morning hours only.

In 1822 Shubert met Weber and Beethoven. Beethoven acknowledged Shubert's genius, but the young Franz showed so much admiration for Beethoven, he requested to be buried next to him.

Shubert died at age 31 from typhoid fever. His music is rich and warm in feelings, spontaneous and passionate. Franz List called him "the most poetic musician ever". He was the most talented songwriter who ever lived, pouring his soul in his lyrical pieces, piano music, symphonies, chamber music, or songs. One might want to listen also to his *Ave Maria.*

12 - THE UNIVERSE

WE ARE PART OF A BIGGER PLAN

This chapter and the next one are a reflection of our place in the Universe, and our connection with it.

As we struggle with our problems every day, we focus on a very limited part of our existence. We think that everything is concentrated on the problem we try to solve, and we see very little of what is around us. This habit which we all have, limits us and brings us to consider only what is there to give us concern and worries. We recoil into ourselves, and we miss what is important.

When I set out writing this book, I intended to write my ideas of how Gentle Therapy could improve all aspects of our lives, and how one can use it at any time.

In this particular situation, what can give us great reassurance and calm our spirits is looking up and *considering the immensity of the Universe, the place we belong to, and notice how insignificant and short lived our problems become.*

Until the 1960's, we thought that the Universe was mainly our Milky Way, and only recently have we discovered that the Universe expands in an immensity of space at a vertiginous speed, and contains billions of other galaxies.

But even before, new ideas about the reality of the Universe were slow to be adopted. Heracleides, a Greek historian, talked about Earth turning on its axis in 350 BC, and Aristarchos of Samos, a Greek astronomer and mathematician, introduced the heliocentric model of our solar system in the year 310 BC, with Earth rotating around the Sun at its center. Those models were dormant for some 1800 years, until Copernicus published in 1543 his book about the Revolution of Celestial Spheres, and were confirmed by Galileo in the 1600's. Galileo, an Italian astronomer, mathematician, and physicist, benefited from the improvements of the telescope, and his observational astronomy caused him to be considered as the "father of modern physics."

Stephen Hawking said: "Galileo, perhaps more than any single person, was responsible for the birth of modern science." In spite of his revolutionary theories, Galileo was forced to deny them because of the Inquisition and lived under house arrest until his death in 1642.

In the scientific world, it was thought that the Universe was fixed and eternal, without a beginning and without an end. Even the illustrious Albert Einstein was convinced for a long time of this eternal and unmovable condition of the Universe, even after he introduced the genius theory of relativity. Einstein arrived through his work to a more personal conclusion and scientific evidence of monotheism, the existence of a single god. He even wrote to a child that: "something, or even better, someone exists behind this immense machinery called the Universe... a spirit immensely superior to man."

Max Planck, who studied the wave duality of light and matter, introduced the quantum theory through his universal constant, or "Planck constant," a purely mathematical discovery, opening the way to Albert Einstein's theory of relativity. Planck said: "all matter originates and exists only by virtue of a force which brings the particle of an atom to vibration and holds this most minute solar system of the atom together. We must assume behind this force the existence of a conscious and intelligent mind. This mind is the matrix of all matter." Because of these beliefs, Planck continued to give lectures on Religion and Science even when he was well in his 80's.

Nevertheless, the idea of a Universe fixed and very stable, with no beginning nor end, eternal, continued to be the standard for many scientists. This was until the theory of the Big Bang was introduced, and later on proved. *Along with the idea of the Big Bang, comes the idea of a beginning of the Universe, and the scientific proof of the Creation, contemplated and supported by many researchers.*

On 21 May 1965, the New York Times announced to the astonished world that "the signals confirmed that the Universe is born as the result of a Big Bang."

This was based on the research and discoveries of Robert Wilson and Arno Penzias made for the Laboratories Bell in a small town of Holmdale, New Jersey. Wilson and Penzias, Doctors in Physics with a specialty in radio-astronomy, were less interested at that time by cosmology, and were in charge of the proper functioning of the antennae capturing the signals of the satellites the Bell company had under contract. They were trying to localize and get rid of a static jamming the emission made by the satellite ECHO, and noticed that the noise was constant, with a stubborn regularity, like an electric wind, universal, creating a cosmic echo.

In 1978, Penzias and Wilson received the Nobel Price for their discovery in cosmic microwave background radiation, but to better understand the immense significance of their ideas, we should take a little detour back to the 1920's, not so far back, when others scientists sensed that the world came from a small particle and then expanded. Since those researchers did not have a way to prove their theories, they were disregarded by the Scientific Societies as unacceptable, and questioning every established principles of cosmology.

The idea of a Universe created from nothing was certainly also bringing in the concept of a plan engendered by an external force, mirrored the Genesis, religious beliefs existing for several millennia. This was not different from the five books of Moses, the Psalms, and the Bible. This would have been too much for the patronizing academia to admit.

This new approach to the theory of the creation of the Universe introduced by modern physicists and astronomers, implicated the idea of a supernatural force that created the Universe from nothing, a unique event generating the very special conditions for the apparition of life, created not only matter, but also time and space to contain life.

In 1992 George Smoot and John Mather, Nobel Price winners in 2006, both physicists, following the information transmitted by the satellite COBE (Cosmic Background Explorer), succeeded to have the images of the most ancient light ever emitted by the early Universe. This was a continuation of the earlier work done by Arno Penzias and Robert Wilson. This archaic, primeval light beam of 13 billions years, was the final proof for the astrophysicists that the Universe had a beginning.

George Smoot declare in front of an electrified audience of the American Society of Physics, in Washington DC, that when he saw for the first time the famous and mysterious images of fine rays present at the edges of the Universe, "it was like contemplating the face of God." Smoot continues to be a professor of physics at the University of Berkeley, California, and more recently, at the Paris Diderot University, France.

Some visionaries ahead of their time had already suggested the idea of a beginning of the Universe and, as one can understand, their theories found no interest from the scientific world of their time. One of them was the great mathematician of the XIX century, Bernhard Riemann, followed by Alexandre Friemann and George Gamow, Russians living during the time of Albert Einstein. Those brilliant researchers worked extensively, during the nights away from their work schedule, making incredibly difficult calculations, convinced that something was wrong with the data of a static Universe.

Around 1922, Alexandre Freeman defied his time by publishing an article in the most respectable journal of his time, Zeitschrift fur Physik, when he introduced the results of his calculations about the beginning of the Universe, originally a simple point which deflated into an expanding Universe. During the same period, Lemaitre, a young abbot from Belgium, was supporting the same idea, and along with Friemann, they fought passionately to convince Einstein to join them in the same conclusion.

One can easily understand that the idea of the entire Universe being contained initially in a single point, without masse, created from a void, as the origin of everything, was hard to be accepted by the scientific world.

The first significant contribution towards proving these new ideas was made by the American astronomer, Edwin Hubble.

Hubble, an accomplished athlete, was a student in Chicago when he won a scholarship to study law in Oxford, England. Eventually, Hubble pursued his passion for studying the sky, became an astronomer, and began working at the Wilson observatory in California.

Here is where Hubble met an extraordinary character, Milton Humason. Humason was a self-taught astronomer who started his career as the mule boy and guardian of the observatory. Eventually his genius was recognized, and his contribution to

Hubble's work helped to achieve one of the most important discoveries of the century.

Until then, the world was believed to be the Milky Way, stable and eternal. Hubble and Humason observed in amazement that there are many other galaxies, billions of them, and they are becoming more distant from each other: the Universe was expanding at an enormous speed! Their discovery was the first direct observation of the Universe to support the Big Bang theory, proposed in 1927 by George Lemaitre.

In addition, Hubble created a system for classifying galaxies, and the expansion of the Universe as shown by the Redshift Distance Law or Hubble Law, helped us to better accept and understand the general model of relativity. This law is based on the idea that the greater the distance between two galaxies, the greater their relative speed of separation, and directly supports the spatial curvature. Hubble was proposed to obtain the Nobel Prize for Physics, honoring his lifetime work, and he would have won it, if he had not died unexpectedly in 1953.

Shortly after the Big Bang, the temperature of the matter, a magma of protons, was extremely hot, of billions of degrees, a burning light made of protons, from which the photons could not escape; the photons, light units, were basically thermic units since they emitted heat only, and practically all was an enormous expansion of energy.

Around 380,000 years after the Big Bang, the temperature of the Universe fell to about 3,000 degrees, and finally, the light could escape, and it is called the primordial. This primordial or the primeval light was the very center of interest of the second part of the XXth century researchers for the signature of the creation, the Primeval Ray. The temperature continued to fall, and now it is close to the absolute zero, 2,7 Kelvin or minus 270 degree.

These first high-energy waves of light emitted very short gamma waves, and progressively losing their energy, slowly fell into infrared waves, then into microwaves. And as Wilson and Penzias demonstrated, those phantoms of primeval light are made now from photons that lost their light and surround us everywhere. In addition, these microwaves are responsible for the constant static found uniformly in the Universe, the signature of first light. The visible photons traveling through the cosmos represent only 4 percent of all the visible photons. Where are the others? They are the ones originating at the dawn of creation, and after traveling more than 13 billion years, became exhausted and totally invisible. But they are omnipresent, creating the baseline noise of the beginning of time.

Another interesting phenomenon to consider is that our Universe is supported by mathematical constants of extraordinary precision; for example, the temperature in the Universe is constant. The three satellites conducting measurements in more and more detail, COBE for George Smoot and John Mather in 1989, WMAP (Wilkinson Microwave Anisotropy Probe) for Charles Bennet in 2001, and PLANCK for Jean-Loup Puget and Jean-Marie Lamarre in 2009. The PLANCK satellite was able to measure back to only a fraction of a billion after the Big Bang (one billionth of a billionth of a billionth of a billionth of a second.)

In January 2010, scientists following PLANCK could give the exact age of the Universe: 13 billion 700 million years. Since March 17, 2010, anyone can see these fantastic images of a detailed chart of the Universe on the ESA website. This allowed Jean-Michel Lamarre, the scientific director of the program to announce on 18 March 2010, that a complete map of the Universe was established when the Universe was only 0,003% of its current age.

Right after the Big Bang, during the period called "inflation," the Universe expanded suddenly at a dizzying speed: every five seconds our Universe increases at a volume equal to the volume of our galaxy, the Milky Way!

Another amazing fact, still a mystery of our Universe, is that "matter" as we see it, accounts only for 4% of the fabric of the Universe, and is made of atoms. 21% of the Universe is black matter, while the remaining 75% is black energy. There is no black color in these entities, but they have been named momentarily so, because we don't know, yet, what they are.

There is more and more a tendency of modern scientists to link the "imaginary time" and black energy to a period *before* the Big Bang. Roger Penrose, George Smoot and Stephen Hawking commented, in different ways, during the last decade, that the expansion of the Universe is an oscillating time, and being somewhat associated with this "phantom energy", or black energy, both considered as being responsible for the Big Bang.

There is so much more to learn about the Universe!

The reader can wonder at this time what all this has to do with Gentle Therapy. Well, several elements can be considered as we learn more and more about the extremely small and the immensely big things contained in this Universe we call home. It is reassuring to know that recent discoveries help us *understand that we belong to a greater plan*, and when isolated and wrapped up in our daily worries as we are, in reality we are part of an extremely larger design.

We are part of a complex and fascinating wholeness, and as the galaxies need the atoms to be created and bound together, so do we humans. *We are also complex in our individuality, disposition, and destiny, while we rest tightly connected and part of our Universe*.

We are not alone, and one should never feel forgotten or neglected, and Gentle Therapy encourages you to take the time and gaze at the sky, reflecting on the immensity, beauty, perfection, and diversity surrounding us.

And if we ever think that we are such a small part of all this vastness, *think of the creation itself:* it started like us, or rather we started like the beginning of the Universe, from the infinitely small, when everything was compressed, crushed into a flake. *This speck without volume gave birth to the infinitely grand*, and with a spark expanded to a grandiose assemblage of stars and planets, galaxies and quasars.

During *your time of meditation include* also a few moments to *consider that you, too, as the Universe contained everything necessary into that initial unimaginable small particle, you are not insignificant, and like our cosmos, you have the potential to grow into something grandiose*.

Furthermore, as part of the Universe uniting us all, it will be good to extend our awareness to other beings and products of nature. It is not only about having respect and admiration for all that surrounds us, but it is important to fraternize with all fellow man, *reaching out, understanding, and helping people less fortunate than us*.

Consider that anyone's condition will ultimately affect ours, sooner or later, from close places or from faraway. Drought, famine, wars, disasters of any nature, injustice, will create an imbalance that will destabilize geographical or political relations, and in the end, will affect our own security.

There is always someone in need of help, and many times we don't have to go far to be able to assist someone. *Maintaining a good balance of the natural offerings presented to us and helping the ones in need, will keep us actively united with our Universe, appreciative, and connected with its divine essence.*

🚲

Special place to consider: **The Grand Canyon.**

One can wonder why majestic places have also a mystical beauty. The Grand Canyon is one of these places, and although it is not as old as the Universe, has an impressive history of a life spanning over millions of years.

The Grand Canyon is part of the Colorado River basin, which dates back 40 million years ago. According to a recent study measuring the age of the Canyon, the lower level of deposits are 1.5 billion years old, and the top layer is 500 million years old, making the canyon many times older than previously thought.

The formation of the Grand Canyon is complex, and includes marine deposits, swamp-like seashores, plateaus made by the elevation of the underground tectonic plaques, and erosions made by the Colorado River. Today, the Grand Canyon measures 277 miles in length, and can be as wide as 18 miles. The Colorado River dug a mile of deep cliffs into the plateau and continues to erode its surface. This process of carving into the different layers of limestone deposits, or old marine sands, resulted in an extraordinarily beautiful landscape of the Canyon. Vast, massive, and majestic, with impressive walls dropping vertiginously, and creating a beautiful variety of colors, the Grand Canyon is a unique and breathtaking place to contemplate.

It is fascinating to learn more about its geology, human history, ethnic population, and customs, and enjoy its beauty. The weather can surprise the visitor with its extremes between summer (as hot as 100 degrees F), and winter (minus 17 degrees F), with daily and altitude variations as well.

There are many plants, trees, and animal life, with species from the East and the West of the country, containing no less than seven life zones. The many parks present include several major ecosystems, allowing a variety in wildlife and temperatures varying from the ones found from Canada to Mexico. For example, three out of four types of deserts found in North America are present here.

This place offers a large variety of activities. Points of interest are many, from many parks and preservation forests and lands, rims of the canyon with waterfalls or steep walls in sheer drops going down 3000 feet in certain places, gorges, and amazing stone formations.

There is a skywalk located on the Hualapai tribal land, in the shape of a horseshoe with a glass floor and projecting 70 feet over the canyon's rim, is a great attraction found on the West side of the Grand Canyon. One can take a railway ride and have an easy but exciting overview of the area, or fly with the eagles and take a helicopter ride.

Tours are offered guiding the tourist on a geological, archeological, photographical, or cultural journey. Native Americans descend from the ancient Pueblo Indians, and today are spread to different corners of the Grand Canyon. One can encounter the Navajo, Sinagua, Walapai, Yuman, or Hualapai people.

Many historic loges, cabins, guesthouses, or desert view watchtowers and hotels can be part of a unique experience while visiting the region.

Millions of years of landscape transformations made by extreme climate changes, and the result of the Colorado River drains and runoffs, fashioned the grounds into incomparable sites. This area is so grandiose and overwhelming in its beauty that it encourages the visitor to stand in silence and reflect on our origins, our planet, and our place in the Universe. The Grand Canyon offers vast and powerful views making the visitor feel like contemplating a cosmic design of faraway constellations.

♫

Music proposed to listen to: **Also sprach Zarathustra (Thus spoke Zarathustra), by Richard Strauss**.

This music, written by Richard Strauss, was inspired by Friedrich Nietzsche's philosophical treatise, *Thus Spoke Zarathustra*. Composed in 1896, the opening *"Sunrise,"* was introduced to a larger public in Stanley Kubrick's film *"2001: A Space Odyssey"* in 1968. It also served to announce the stage entrance for Elvis Presley.

The main character is *Zarathustra*, a fictional prophet known in the ancient Persian culture as *Zoroaster*. Zoroaster promoted a doctrine of morality and high human values and served as a model for Nietzsche's story.

It is believed that Nietzsche, who was walking on a wooded mountain in Switzerland near the lake of Silvaplana, was struck by the sight of a gigantic rock formation. He had the strong impression that an ancient prophet, *Zarathustra,* was speaking to him with a powerful will. *Zarathustra* undergoes transfiguration and embraces eternity, while living his legacy to men to perpetuate his aspirations. From there, Nietzsche built a human being transitioning through morality and truthfulness, to a more idealistic metaphysical realm. He sees man as becoming a superman "achieving self-mastery, self-cultivation, self-direction, and who wants deep eternity."

In Ecce Homo, Nietzsche writes that: "With *Thus Spoke Zarathustra*, I have given mankind the greatest present that has ever been made so far. This book, with a voice bridging centuries, is not only the highest book there is, the book that is characterized by the air of heights – it is also the deepest, born out of the innermost wealth of truth, an inexhaustible well to which no pail descends without coming up again filled with gold and goodness."

The musical arrangement made by Richard Strauss is dramatic and compelling; the *"Dawn"* or the *"Nature"* motif, made of five notes, announces the beginning of this symphonic poem, and is repeated throughout this work in overtone series. The philosophical implications of Richard Strauss' art are represented by contrasting themes interacting in a spectacular opposition; one written in B major represents Humanity, and the other in C major represents the Universe. Those two tonalities, which are adjacent to each other, are present in the final section of the poem, and, played together, create an impression of discordance.

Defined as the "World Riddle Theme" these two conflicting keys ending together, suggest that the speech of Zarathustra will not solve the riddle. As the dialog between humanity and its universe will not end, so close but so much confronting each other, so will stand their never ending dialogue.

It is interesting to note that other composers found inspiration in the work of Nietzsche; Gustav Mahler in his Third Symphony, and Frederick Delius who wrote a three-movement composition.

Richard Strauss' work will transport any audience into a world of supreme inspiration with his magnificent and powerful romanticism.

13 - CONNECTING WITH THE DIVINE

In the preceding chapter we were talking about being part of a bigger plan, our Universe. We also reflected on the work of some scientists that introduced the concept of the world being created from nothing, a simple point infinitely small and without volume.

Although religions of all origins, and existing since the dawn of time, were based on the belief of a divinity governing the heavens, science brings in surprising proofs of a superior plan that created our Cosmos, and questions how, why, and from where the Universe was created.

The Big Bang theory is all about Creation, although in reality there was not Big, all staring from a minute point, and no Bang, since there was nothing around, no matter nor air, to make the initial explosion resonate. The Big Bang theory conciliates in our modern times the biblical beliefs with science. Bringing revolutionary ideas based on the recent discoveries, science makes peace with religion in the historic rivalry for supremacy controlling humanity as to how to look at the Universe. *This should make anyone feel in harmony with science and religion*; there is no need to make a choice on the way we consider ourselves in this world, for *one can be a highly spiritual person and at the same time marvel at the scientific perfection of our existence.*

As a confirmation of the scriptures, the astronomers and physicists established the evidence that in the beginning was this unique point, of an unexplained origin, expanding to create the Universe with its billions of stars and galaxies. George Gamow, renowned Russian scientist, writing his book "The creation of the Universe" in1944, calls the era preceding the Big Bang, this mysterious pre-material era "the era of Saint Augustine." Indeed, in the 4th century, Augustine then Christian and philosopher, wrote: "the Universe is not born in time, it is born *with* the time." Some 1500 years later, Albert Einstein would make a similar statement. Other scientists think that the Universe was created by the Big Bang, but the laws, the forces that made it happen existed *before.*

Science began debating the idea of an era before the Big Bang, before time, before space, and before matter. This approach links religious thinking to very precise scientific measurements.

One would wonder about this fantastic energy suddenly flooding from an infinitely small point into the void, containing the potential of organizing itself into well-defined systems such as galaxies and clusters. Furthermore, having the natural disposition to evolve from inert mineral formations, into organized molecules, then, through a continuous progress of life, becoming complex functional organisms.

This process perfecting the living organisms is responsible for producing genetic codes contained in the cells and capable of transmitting information encoded in its DNA. The natural progression, like a mysterious design, astounding in its magnificence and majestic beauty, continues producing intelligent creatures, evolving into thinking beings, having a mind and a conscience of their own.

This makes the American astro-physician, Robert Jastrow, write in his book "The science and the Creation" that "finally the astronomers and the cosmologists found themselves face to face with theologians, who always thought that what we could call a supernatural force, a creative force, is responsible of what happened at the origin of the world."

Reflecting on the universal constants, real wonders of the nature found by the physicists and mathematicians, going beyond their findings, they question the reason for all this. Stephen Hawking, the English astro-physicist, writes: "the lows of science, as we know them presently, contain certain fundamental numbers, such as the electrical charge of the electron, or the masse of a proton and electron. What is remarkable is that the value of these numbers has been very finely adjusted in order to make development of life possible."

In the 80's, scientists are ranging in two groups, some like Joseph Silk in Oxford, supporting the older idea of a fixed cosmos, and others like Stephen Hawking in Cambridge and Roger Penrose in Oxford, introducing the Singularity - a mathematic point at the origin of the Universe – and becoming a community described as "the face of God".

The fundamental constants, also named as the "violent coincidences", govern the laws of the Universe without which stars, life, and humans could not exist.

For example, if one second after the Big Bang, the expansion would have been 1% slower, the cosmos would have collapsed in it self; it would have been 1% faster, and the stars could not have formed.

The law of nuclear attraction makes protons and neutrons stay glued solidly together in the nucleus of an atom; Stephen Hawking observes that: "if this nuclear force had been very slightly elevated, the fusion of the hydrogen would have become impossible, and life as we know it would not exist."

Cosmological conclusions and philosophical considerations derived from quantum physics made Fritjeaf Capra think that there is a parallel between modern physics and ancient Eastern philosophies. Capra thinks that the metaphysical beliefs of the Oriental scriptures found in Chinese Taoism and Buddhist Sutras describing a "divine principle" of our Universe, preceded the work of modern physicists.

Physicists demonstrated that individual particles of an atom are held in a relationship that cannot be naturally separated from the nucleus. The atom as unit of matter is made of a multiplicity of things, as matter is many things and one thing at the same time.

One can only wonder about all these mysterious physical constants, all expressed in mathematical figures, extremely precise and constant: the speed of light, gravitational constant, electronic masse, and ultimately, the cosmological constant or "Number of Planck." This number is the index that measures the relation between energy radiated and the frequency of the wave emitted, which is a 0, followed by 119 zeros then 1! This is of a mind-blowing precision if we consider this universal constant at the time of the formation of the cosmos.

In order for the galaxies to take form, any slight deviation in either direction would have made their existence impossible. Planck, who already introduced the "Time of Planck" as the smallest fraction of time that can ever be calculated at the time of the Big Bang, was awarded with the Nobel Price in 1918!

Another interesting coincidence is that the size of man is equal to the radius of Earth multiplied by the radius of the atom, and the masse of a human is equal to the masse of Earth multiplied by the masse of the atom.

In this world there is a natural tendency, called by the astro-physicist Fred Hoyle, a "coup monte" of the nature to organize spontaneously from the very simple elements into more complex systems. Ilya Prigogine, Nobel price of chemistry in 1977, dedicated many years of his research to show this natural tendency of inert material to organize into stars, planets, and galaxies. This way, simple formations of minerals, then organic structures, progress naturally toward a very complex living material. Prigogine senses that the matter has: "a tendency to auto structure itself to become living matter".

In the same note, Hoyle says: "the more I analyze the Universe and study the details of its architecture, the more I found proofs that the Universe "knew" that humans would have to appear. There are astonishing examples of the lows of nuclear physics that seem to conspire to create the Universe inhabitable."

Hawking, Freeman, and Dyson made also the observation that the formation of more complex structures ultimately lead to life, as we know it on Earth.

Modern scientists are talking of a "spiritual" entity governing the architecture and the functioning of the Universe. In 1936 Albert Einstein was already thinking that "all of the people who are seriously involved in science will end one day by understanding that a spirit is manifested in the laws of the Universe, a spirit immensely more superior to man."

All of which brings us to believe that there must be a purpose for the existence of the world, and for our existence as well. We live in a era of great discoveries, but also of new spiritual enlightening, and it is fascinating that we have the privilege to bring to our inquiring minds, and into our faithful hearts, a new harmony, made possible by the new scientific information. One can clearly notice that there is a strong metaphysic implication present in the world of scientific research today.

So what does all this have to do with Gentle Therapy? Well, it only brings in the idea that it is good to connect with the Universe. Simply *staying in touch and feeling more secure* knowing that we belong to something greater than our minuscule physical appearance. It is reassuring to feel the gentle embrace of this complex and superb system we belong to evolving and changing continually.

Staying attuned with our Universe means also learning more about it, wander at the immensity, beauty, and the fine orchestration of its functioning. As the great minds of all times continue to ponder the infinite complexity and spiritual purpose of our Universe, *we experience a connection to a higher level* if we pursue our own quest for understanding our own place within it.

Bringing closer to us these reflections of the presence of superior forces and trying to *connect to the divine*, should be so much more comforting to consider that *we are surrounded by the gentle presence of a divine grace*, and that if we look closely, we will find it everywhere. I can imagine the same grace casting a spell when Albert Einstein was playing the violin, while Max Planck was sitting at the piano, and they enjoyed playing together for hours, without talking. It probably was the same divine grace that inspired them during sleepless nights of intense and exhausting calculations and research.

I truly believe that the real Gentle Therapy is to *see and connect with the divine anywhere and anytime. Letting the light of the Creation pour into your soul*, especially when you feel lost or down, *will fill you with the divine energy stronger than any other power,* stronger than any evil force. You don't have to do much, *just choose God, and let the good energy work for you*, once you made this conscious allegiance.

When you worry about material things or events in life, think that this can be only the part of things seen, which is in many cases elusive. The unseen is most of the time the "real" thing; consider that light is made of a spectrum of many colors, and every thing in the nature absorbs only certain colors of the spectrum reflecting the others: so what we see is the color that is rejected, the only color that the object is not. If we see the grass green, in reality is all but green, as the sky is all but blue. When everything is white, without color, in reality all the colors are present and blend together!

So, why not trust our most fundamental instincts telling us that there is a lot more to what we observe, that we can find beauty and goodness in simple ways of life and places?

We all benefit from *taking the time to look around*, marvel at the smallest creature, plant, or land configuration, or take a larger look at the sky. That should bring not only peace and happiness into our minds, but connect us with the creator of all there is.

Take the time to marvel at the infinity of designs found in simple snowflakes, the beauty, perfection, and variety of small or grandiose things found in nature. *Try to find God at every step you make. You will feel serene and protected.*

I can see God in a situation like the one described by a reporter traveling in a refugee camp in Africa. At the end of a long line distributing food, a little girl coming from faraway accompanied by two smaller children, was waiting patiently her turn. When the little girl and her brothers finally made it to the table, the only item left was a single banana. The young girl, instead of being disappointed, took the banana, peeled it, and gave one half to each of her brothers; then sitting on the side of the road, she started happily to leak the banana peel. In our world, where we are so spoiled or so blessed, seeing a person so much more deprived and not complaining, but appreciating such a little gift, in my mind was like seeing God in its all-simple appreciation.

I see God in the gentle face of a mother watching her child, and the smile of the baby when she hovers over him.

I see God in a homeless person returning a wallet filled with money to its proprietor.

I saw God every time I delivered a baby, another miracle of creation, never being able to stop these tears of deep emotions of happiness and wonder.

I see God in any creature caring for their offspring, any flower opening its petals, every sunset I admire from my daily walk on the pier.

And I see God in every loving look in somebody's face.

Gentle Therapy *is about seeing everywhere this free and superb gift of the divine that surrounds us*: it is up to us to see it, discover it, and enjoy it.

Connecting with the Divine is about keeping this therapeutic, gentle, and profound connection with the natural gifts of the Universe. It is about benefiting from the splendor of nature, from our Universe, include it in our life at every moment, become part of it, cherish it, and share it with others.

🚲

Place to visit: **Mountain of Beatitudes.**

The mountain of Beatitudes is believed to be the place where Jesus Christ gave his first important speech, and it is located on a hill overlooking the See of Galilee near Capernaum.

According to Matthew 5:1, Jesus "seeing the multitudes, went up into a mountain: and when He was set, his disciples came unto Him: And He open His mouth, and thought them, saying":

"Blessed are the poor in spirit; for theirs is the kingdom of heaven.

Blessed are they that mourn; for they shall be comforted. ...

Blessed are the merciful; for they shall obtain mercy.

Blessed are the pure at heart; for they shall see God.

Blessed are the peacemakers; for they shall be called the children of God. ...

Rejoice, and be exceedingly glad; for great is your reward in heaven".

Matthew 5:3-12 "The sermon of The Beatitudes":

"And a great multitude of people out of all Judea and Jerusalem, and from the sea coast of Tyre and Sidon, which came to hear him, and to be healed of their diseases," Matthew 5:2.

Luke describes in his text on Jesus' sermon before the multitude: "And they that were vexed with unclean spirits: they were healed. And the whole multitude sought to touch Him: for there went virtue out of Him, and healed them all. And He lifted up his eyes on His disciples, and said, *Blessed be ye poor: for yours is the kingdom of God".*

The word Beatitudes has its origin from the Latin "Beati" – blessed, and it is the first section of the moral teachings contained in the sermon. Many Christians consider the Sermon on the Mount as a form of reintroduction of the Ten Commandments, and it ends as the first presentation of the *Lord's Prayer.*

The Mountain of Beatitudes is today a place of pilgrimage, and one can visit a church, a monastery, gardens, and paths connecting each other and close by holy places. The whole area is beautiful, as one can expect, but the serenity and peaceful atmosphere inspired by this place make anyone feel in touch with the divine, and one can understand why Jesus found this place so unique.

Jesus went to Capernaum, a close by Roman city, when he was not well accepted back in his home city, Nazareth, and made Capernaum his second native city. It was also Peter's hometown, and was a busy city with trade of silk, spices, and other goods located on the road to Damascus. Here Jesus performed many of the miracles described in the New Testament. Visiting Capernaum, one can see a Synagogue built next to a Roman Temple by the centurion whose servant was healed by Jesus (Luke 7). The place contains Jewish and Roman stone ruins covered with carved symbols designing palms, the Star of David, the Menorah, and the Ark of Covenant. The first Christians also venerated this place as one of the places Jesus worshipped and healed.

Peter's house cannot be missed, it is close to the temple, and was a large structure for its time, hosting many of the disciples when they had to escape persecution after Jesus' crucifixion. It is a round structure, well preserved, and to my great surprise, from the ground level where the house stands, one is unaware of the gentle transition to come when going to the next level. Above it is built a church, with windows all around inviting inside the breathtaking views of the See of Galilee. The floors are of glass, and it brings the heart of the church of Christ above the House of Peter.

Although the church was built recently, the two structures are in perfect harmony, and standing inside, one is engulfed by a sentiment of eternal mystery.

The Mount of the Beatitudes and Capernaum are located in a larger area of the North side of the See of Galilee; the whole area is of striking beauty, and contains many of the places where Jesus went to find inspiration and start preaching. Visiting these places I could understand how one can get so close to God.

♬

Music of inspiration: **Sacred Treasures I,** orthodox choral music selection from classical music, edited by Hearts of Space. This is a collection of classical compositions by musicians such as Rachmaninov, Tchaikovsky, and Anton written in the tradition of the Russian liturgy, with angelic voices singing *a capella.* This deeply moving music would make anyone feel connected with the heavens, and can serve as an excellent background for moments of meditation.

Following the same strongly emotional atmosphere, I would like to recommend **"The Prayer Cycle" by Jonathan Elias.** Elias, an American composer for television and films, wrote "The Prayer Cycle" in 1999, as a collection of nine Adagio poems, and as he states, he tried to create a feeling of cross-cultures. Elias considers that music opens people's hearts, and it is a great chance for people to heal. "The Prayer Cycle" is written in twelve languages, and has as titles: Merci, Strength, Hope, Compassion, Innocence, Forgiveness, Benediction, and Faith. Elias describes his music as a spiritual, survival music, a global music for peace and forgiveness, music to heal each other. When listening to this poignant music, we are transported across distances, times, and cultural differences, and we all blend as children of the same planet.

"Music produces a kind of pleasure which human nature cannot do without"

$\qquad\qquad\qquad\qquad\qquad\qquad$ *Confucius.*

14 - MUSIC THERAPY

Music is another element of life, another dimension of human expression besides words and thoughts. Music accompanies our happy and dramatic events, and is present when words can no longer represent our feelings.

Music ability to evoke a multitude of emotions, in their more subtle nuances, gives us a different chance to experience an infinite variety of sentiments in a very unique way. Music can make us feel happy or immensely sad, and plays as a background for a variety of activities or events.

One can find musical individuality in all cultures, styles, and historical periods. Children are raised, educated, or cradled to sleep with the help of music, while young ones are surrounded by their own style of music, even if not always appreciated by the grownups.

Music is such an intrinsic part of our life that one cannot imagine a party, sport event, or even an exercise class without it. We travel now with our headphones on, wrapped up in our own world; we do the homework and house chores encouraged by the bit of the music. We could not conceive watching a movie without the dramatic support of the musical scores that amplify the mood and the action.

Be it instrumental, vocal, or both, everyone can find the type and genre that fits one's taste and predilection. It is rare to know someone who has never whistled, sang in the shower, or joined in for a song. It is just an essential human need of inner emotional manifestation.

The same need to bring music into play was seen since ancient times, and music was present during a variety of private or public events. Magical texts containing incantations made by Chaldean doctors were found in a royal cemetery in the city of Ur in Babylon. Some other discoveries found descriptions made by Hebrews, in the middle of the 4th millennium B.C., portrayed musicians paying the harp, cithara, tympanon, and double flute.

Hittites, Syrians, Babylonians, and Persians left numerous artifacts behind, such as the written fragments in cuneiform alphabet about the musical scale used some 2,800 B.C. and six melodies to God Enlil found in the city of Nippur. In tombs in Syria and Babylon were found multiple models of harps and lyres, dating from 2,700 B.C. Bas-reliefs in Persia depict dancers and musicians attending a ceremonial cult of Mithras and Cybele.

Egypt's national instrument is the harp, and its existence has been described or found in tombs 3,500 years B.C., with harps having 7 to 11 strings. The cult of Amon-Ra, the Sun-King, was celebrated with dancers, singers, and musicians playing harps, luths, double flutes, and citharas.

In the Greek culture, the harp is also present along with tambourines, cymbals, and flutes. Apollo, the god of arts and beauty, was recognized as playing the lyre, as was Orpheus. In ancient Greece the presence of music was always encountered in the amphitheatres playing tragedies.

Eastern European and Middle Eastern countries developed another type of musical expression of Christianity, besides the local folk music. Constantine 1st, then Justinian, and other emperors of the Byzantine Empire followed the model introduced by Jean Chrysostom in the Orthodox liturgy, during the Syrian mass in Antioch.

Music has been present in descriptions of heaven, where angels delight the lucky inhabitants by playing harps, lyres, flutes, and other instruments.

I encourage the use of Music as Gentle Therapy for the soothing effects it has on our mood and our health. It is customary to find a musical background in beauty parlors and spas because of its relaxing effects, and music is recommended by therapists to help people to distress, find sleep, or meditate.

Looking at music from its therapeutic aspects, music has and is largely used in helping or healing numerous conditions. Because *music has such an impact on our physical, emotional, mental, social, and spiritual life*, music therapy can improve all these aspects of our existence. Professionals involved in Music Therapy can be psychologists, physicians, and physical and occupational therapists. Some psychologists are studying the effects of music therapy on our intellect and behavior.

In more modern times Music Therapy was offered by both professionals and amateurs, after World War II, when therapists volunteered to play at Veterans' Hospitals for injured soldiers around the country, and helped them recover from physical and emotional traumas. The impact of Music Therapy on improving Veterans medical recovery was such, that doctors insisted on hiring musicians for the hospitals to assist them in their treatments.

Thus, the first Music Therapy program in the world was founded in 1944 at Michigan State University. The American Music Therapy Association was officially opened in 1994. There is a national examination after completing the degree, offering a Certification by the Board of Music Therapists. Since 1994 Medicare recognized Music Therapy as a service under the Partial Hospitalization Programs (PHP), and is reimbursable under certain conditions: must be prescribed by a doctor, necessary for the treatment of that particular illness or injury, and goals established and proven efficient.

Music therapy can be used as a proficient tool *in schools, hospitals, nursing homes, private therapy offices, and by any person for personal benefits.*

In hospitals, music is used as a complement to help control pain and depression, to calm, and to sedate. By relaxing muscles and psychological tension, music can help to induce sleep. For *patients with mental problems, music can positively change aggressive moods or anxiety, control responses and actions, counteract fear and apprehension, and improve relations.*

In schools, musical practice is not only considered a pleasant curriculum, but *teaches students to focus, improve their coordination skills, helps to learn how to work in a group while listening the to other players, in addition to being exposed to a new form of artistic expression.*

Music therapy exercises benefits to our health; researches have shown that even the brain waves follow the musical tempo: when faster, it sharpens our concentration and speed, when slower, promotes a calm and meditative state. Upon the changes of brain wave speed, a response of the autonomic nervous system is observed, altering accordingly the heart and breathing rate.

Through music intervention, therapists can improve a patient's cognitive and motor functions, and social and communication skills. People who are still professionally active learn how to process various tasks and how to relax, and the elderly benefit by improving their orientation and memory. Stroke patients and patients with mental illnesses such as depression and melancholia, can improve when listening to music.

Music, by inducing a positive state of mind, reduces chronic stress, and, by keeping at bay depression and anxiety, ultimately prevents heart attacks and strokes. Basically, *music can become another important tool in maintaining a good health.*

In my own experience as a Physical Medicine and Rehabilitation Doctor, I have tried in some cases of patients afflicted with aphasia, a condition preventing the patient to speak, to have him/her listen to a popular melody, and observed that they had no trouble picking up that melody and singing along. This is because the brain's structural representation of a melodic text is situated in a different location of the cortex, which in many instances was not damaged by the stroke.

Besides using *Music Therapy as a way of relaxation, or enjoyment, music can be a magnificent tool to transport us into the world of our imagination.* Although music is part of our common life, it can be present as a 'parallel dimension', a different and more abstract manner of expression of our feelings and emotions. In the era when scientists are studying the concept of parallel universes, or even of multiverses (a place where multiple universes coexist together), in the physical condition of this present life, we can conceive the possibility of a multitude of ways we envision our world. *Music can become a mode of controlling emotions, creativity, and a way of communicating with and understanding our souls.*

Most musicians passionately dedicate their time and lives to performing or creating musical pieces. They are consumed by the need to reproduce in sounds, at times with great difficulty, using waves and vibrations, what they live intensely in their imaginary world. Ludwig van Beethoven, who consecrated his life to composing music, noticed his hearing declining as a young adult and that he was rapidly loosing his ability to hear the real sounds. There could not have been anything more devastating for his genius then being deprived from hearing his own art. However, he continued to listen and compose his best masterpieces in his imaginary world, aided by the power of his abstract representation of music.

Music is a perfect example of transforming our thoughts into reality, bringing the mental representation of emotions into the real world of sounds, then returning to reactivate these emotions through musical reverberation. At this point, *music is felt by our body as vibrations, and by our soul as emotions. It is the connection between physical and abstract existential representations; it is the embodiment of sensations.*

Because of the *high mental activity stimulated by music, it is important to think of exposing children, from early age,* and possibly as early as being in the womb, to music, and in particular to classical music. The fetus is able to hear sounds, voices, mother's heartbeat, noises, and music. It is important to pay attention to what kind of sounds we expose our babies to, even before their birth, considering that music plays a significant part in the brain development of the fetus.

Scientists estimate that the human brain creates near to 2 million synapses, or neural connections, per second beginning the second month of gestation. This process will continue and by age of three a child could have made up to 1,000 trillion synapses. What these connections will be depends on the stimulations the child has been exposed to, and is different for each future human being. A child recognizes music heard in the womb, and calms down if mother's heartbeat is played. In some childcare places in Europe, it is customary to use this mode of calming small infants, by recording the baby's mother's heart sounds and playing them when she is not there.

More importantly, the plasticity of the brain from early age, in creating multiple connections based on the stimuli the baby is exposed to, can influence his choices and personality later in life. The adult a child will become depends on the way that child has been raised and to the infinity of influences he has been exposed to.

When a child is raised in an environment lacking parental attention, directions, or discipline, is the same as if he is lacking food and love, and he will likely have less academic success, a higher risk to drop out of school, or become delinquent. On the contrary, children raised in more stable familial structures, have better social skills, self-discipline, and manners. If they are rewarded for their accomplishments and their efforts are recognized, they have a better chance to succeed. These children seem to go more often to college, have a higher interaction with others, and there is a higher possibility of becoming a prominent figure of society. This brings in the idea that we build our ideals from the cultural influences and people we came in contact with.

A person will build his character from his experience of reality, and this will influence his imagination, dreams, and feelings, stored by neural connections of billion synapses since childhood. We all build and reinforce certain pathways and we extinguish others, and this very complicated network, as complex as the Universe itself, will determine who we are. Thus, our particularities, our memories, expectations, interests, preferences, and experiences, all are contributing to making us very different, very unique as a person.

The music we expose our children to is an intense stimulation and can greatly contribute to the formation of a more complex neurological network.

This will influence the molding of a future person, and the complexity of the neural integrations of environmental influences and experiences, will affect the ability to connect, express feelings, and the values which establish directions in life.

Our future choices will be the result of these influences and will determine what we want to be in the future and how we see ourselves in connection with others and the Universe.

Applying music as *Gentle Therapy is, like in all the other chapters of this book, including the benefits of music in our daily life*. I discovered the therapeutic influence of music without even knowing it, and for a long time now, I use it as my favorite "psychotherapy."

I grew up with music and I soon chose the harp as my favorite instrument. My mother inspired me by playing an old instrument at home, symbolizing for me the ideal of grace and beauty.

Little by little I considered music as a future career. I was attending concerts, operas, and recitals as often as I possibly could, and engulfed myself into the magical world of music. I grew passionate about the great artists and interpreters, and I tried to penetrate their secrets of mastering vocal and instrumental techniques to the highest levels. Fascinated by composers, I learned about different styles and manners of musical expressions. And I also learned that a great art of interpretation comes with intense dedication to relentless practice, aspiring to achieve perfection, and the ability to sacrifice play, vacation, and holidays. Basically I learned that I could no longer be a child if I committed to devote my attention and time to a musical career.

Music became my dearest friend, my passion, and my therapy. It consoled me when I felt lonely or misunderstood by others, it opened a magical dimension of harmony and beauty, making me feel transported to Heaven. Music gave me strength and courage to continue to play better and longer, it inspired me in my interpretations, translating my emotions and ideas. It gave me discipline and understanding that music, just as any other performing art, requires perfection at the first trial, since one cannot go back and correct a mistake already made while playing in public. I found that music has strict architectural forms, sounds that are made of harmonical waves responding to physical laws, and that composers applied a rigorous mathematical structure to their art.

Later on I understood how much music helped me in life: when studying medicine I already had engraved in me the practice of exactitude and precision, the capacity of intense mental concentration for long periods of time, and a memory trained for intricate details occurring simultaneously. It is why I recommend *music as a great practice for children, not only as a pleasant activity and for its calming effects, but also for teaching discipline and accuracy in performing everything else in life.*

When I was performing at the Symphony in Monte Carlo and expecting my daughter Beatrice, she was exposed to a great amount of musical stimulations. From my own practice, or from the waves of vibrations coming from the orchestra, Beatrice was surrounded and entertained by beautiful sounds. She grew up happy and well balanced, surprising every one from the Symphony with her spontaneous reproduction of melodies from the most difficult pieces of music, such as Richard Wagner. It was quite a spectacle to see my fellow colleagues surprised look when my toddler was following heartedly the melody of "The Ride of the Valkyries."

Later on, at her turn, Beatrice made sure to listen often to classical music when she became pregnant, and during that time I enjoyed making soothing playlists of her favorite composers. One day when Beatrice and I were talking on the videophone, she asked me to look at Alexandre, my grandson; he was watching Baby Beethoven from the series Baby Einstein, singing out loud and "directing" with passion The Symphony No 5; he was just a little over one year old!

Music continues to be my favorite Gentle Therapy, and coming home from a busy day, there is no better way for me to unwind than playing the harp. It calms me, transports me to a peaceful world, and quickly everything seems more simple and natural; at once I feel more refreshed and ready to go on with my daily activities.

I recommend to anyone to appeal to the therapeutic effects of music; *learning to play a musical instrument or singing in a choir is so personally rewarding* and without the pressures of having to perform professionally. It is a true joy to share a nice tune with others, so join in as loud as you can, and have fun!

⍈

Place to visit

Choosing the place of our voyage was somewhat difficult, because there are so many places where music has been highly regarded; Vienna as the place where great composers such as Mozart, Beethoven, Schubert, Brahms, Haydn, Johann Strauss Sr. and Jr., Schonberg lived, and where the famous Vienna Philharmonic Orchestra performs. Bayreuth hosts Wagner Festival, Salzburg is known for its Mozart Festival, while many other cities offer exceptional musical events. Paris, London, Rome, Milan, New York, and Chicago represent only a few places of choice when it comes to musical art celebration.

Bravely biased I settled for the **Principality of Monaco,** this fairytale place where real princes and princesses live, and where French and Italian cultures blend, under a climate and geographical conditions favored by gods. Monaco is the world's second smallest state, after the Vatican, and has a population of roughly 16,000 fitting in some three quarters of a square mile. Situated on the French Riviera, 10 miles from Italy, Monaco is a principality governed by the House of Grimaldi since 1297. There is a distinction between Monaco the City, located on the Rock of Monaco, and the State of Monaco, containing four distinctive areas: Monaco-Ville, La Condamine, Monte Carlo and Fontvieille.

Although Monaco is ruled by one of the Grimaldi princes, since 1911 under the Treaty of Versailles, Monaco benefits from French protection, as it surrounds this State on three sides, the fourth being the Mediterranean Sea.

Monaco is the place where an American actress became princess, where the climate and architectural styles are magnificent, the views are breathtaking, and life seems easy and exciting. Monaco is clean and safe like Switzerland, green and lush like a botanical garden, offering gambling places like Las Vegas, elegant and sophisticated like the beaches of Saint Tropez...

Rich in culture, sport events, sumptuous hotels, and casinos, Monaco is a tax haven, not imposing any taxes or income on individuals. Monaco is about an hour from the South Alps' slopes, hosts the Formula One Monaco Grand Prix, and sponsors numerous charity events for UNICEF and other organizations. Monaco has its own Monegasque coin along with the use of the euro, although is not a part of the European Union.

Tourism is one of its main sources of income and people come by air, land, and sea to this ideally situated harbor. Banking, telecommunications, and high-value non-polluting industries are present. Main attractions are the Oceanographic Museum, the casinos, superb stores and jewelers, and the botanical garden. But one can just wander in the streets of Monaco or Monte Carlo and be enchanted by the colors, light, and stylish vibration of this magical place.

The Grand Casino is well known and a hallmark in Monte Carlo, but what remains a little more secretive is that the Monte Carlo Opera is contained inside the Casino. Built in 1858 as a project by Garnier, the architect commissioned to build the Opera in Paris, Monte Carlo Opera is a veritable jewel box for the princes. It became an attraction aided by the construction of the French Railroad connecting Paris to Monaco. More recently a new, larger concert hall, was conveniently located in the Monte Carlo Sporting Club and Casino, but I will always keep close to my heart the memories of the concerts and operas I had the privilege to attend as part of the orchestra performing in the older building. We were all transported by the presence of Princess Grace, a passionate supporter of music and arts, and waited for her to enter the royal box before starting the performance.

I had the great pleasure to be part of presentations of the most illustrious musicians of the time, great soloists and singers, under the direction of well-known conductors, such as Igor Markevitch, the musical Director of that period.

In summertime, the Monte Carlo Orchestra participated in the Monaco Summer Festival, performed in the Palace's courtyard. It was an event highly anticipated and regally attended, but for we musicians, it was a challenge, since the humidity present in the month of August made difficult maintaining the proper tuning and fighting droplets formed on the instruments.

Monaco is a truly unique place by its location, climate, and culture, and assembles in a very small space the highest concentration of activities, entertainment, and beautiful surroundings.

♫

Music I recommend for this chapter is a piece of **harp music**, and a variety of choices are between **Debussy** (Claire de Lune), **Mozart** (Concerto for flute, harp and orchestra), **Boieldieu** (Concerto for Harp), and many others. But a shorter, although difficult solo harp piece of music that I enjoy sometimes to sit down and play, is the **Passacaglia by Handel**.

Born in Halle, Germany, in 1685, Georg Friedrich Haendel who later in life adopted the British spelling of George Frideric Handel, shares the same year of birth with Johann Sebastian Bach and Domenico Scarlatti. Handel developed his talents under the influence of German and Italian baroque music, and extended his interests to polyphonic choral traditions. Handel composed oratorios and operas when he was in Florence at the invitation of Ferdinando de Medici, and his famous *Dixit Domine* dates from this period.

Handel is well known for his *Water Music, Music for the Royal Fireworks*, and *Messiah*, all written in England where he settled in 1712, and lived the rest of his life.

Passacaglia, a more modest work, is a piece of music that has an introduction, called the theme, followed by variations written in such a way that the theme remains always easy to recognize. Handel wrote many small lovely melodies during his prolific career, and it seems that the harp was one of his favorite instruments. And harp players definitely love his music.

"I tell you the truth, if you have faith as small as a mustard seed, you can say to this mountain: Move from here to there and it will move. Nothing will be impossible for you."

Jesus Christ in Matthew 17:20.

15 - PRAYER THERAPY

The Lord is my Shepherd...
That's Relationship!

I shall not want...
That's Supply!

He maketh me to lie down in green pastures...
That's Rest!

He leadeth me beside the still waters...
That's Refreshment!

He resoreth my soul...
That's Healing!

He leadeth me in the paths of righteousness...
That's guidance!

For His name sake...
That's Purpose!

Yea, though I walk through the valley of the shadow of death...
That's Testing!

I will fear no evil...
That's Protection!

For Thou art with me...
That's Faithfulness!

Thy rod and Thy staff they comfort me...
That's Discipline!

Thou preparest a table before me in the presence of mine enemies...
That's Hope!

Thou annointest my head with oil...
That's Consecration!

My cup runneth over...
That's Abundance!

Surely goodness and mercy shall follow me all the days of my life...
That's Blessing!

And I will dwell in the house of the Lord...
That's Security!

For ever...
That's Eternity!

"The 23rd Psalm" - Author unknown

Since the beginning of time, prayer has been a way of communicating with God. Prayer is a strong emotional expression of our requests to higher and more powerful authority. It is universally recognized as a deep need to appeal, particularly in times of trouble, to supreme entities influencing our existence from other realms. Prayer has been present as part of cultural and spiritual expression in all societies, no matter how primitive or undeveloped.

In all parts of the planet, different religions have their own prayer practices, and all are manifested through strong beliefs in the power of prayer. Prayer is practiced regularly by millions of adepts of Buddhism, Hinduism, Judaism, Taoism, Christians, New Age, along with many others forms of spiritual and secular traditions.

Prayer is an innate part of the humankind, and made as a reflex action, or as an intended request for help, prayer is this urge, hard to explain, to address our most intimate pleas to the supernatural powers. But what we know, or what we experience at times, is that prayers work.

Prayer is also a privilege. It is the key to open the door to the holy places, to open a communication with God. This privilege was reserved in the past to a very few, when the priests were the only ones allowed to enter the Holy of the Holies. Holy of the Holies represents the inner sanctuary of temples and churches, as the very restricted and most sacred places found in most religions, past and present.

Originally, in Judaism the Holy of the Holies was the Tabernacle within the Temple in Jerusalem, shielded and containing the Ark of the Covenant, and was entered only by the High Priest, and only once a year at Yom Kippur. In the Christian religion, the Altar is considered the Holy Place, and certain priests and deacons entered or touched the Holy Doors or the Holy Table, and during specific times of the mass only. Very few exceptions were allowed, such as the Russian Tsar on the day of coronation, after the anointing, and accompanied by the Patriarch of all Orthodox churches. When the priests were entering the Holy of the Holies, they had to announce their coming by ringing a bell, and were attached by a cord, symbol of their attachment to earthy life to which they had to come back.

Nowadays, we enter this spiritual sanctuary through prayer, and bring our praise and petitions to God, as prayer opens the entrance to Heaven. Over the centuries, clergymen, ordinary men, and believers in a new spiritual awareness, insisted on the value and the need to pray. And even non-believers make prayers in times of need.

Prayer, in our modern society, is still present and has known resurgence for the last decades. One example is Samuel Prime who was, among other ministers, influencing a new wave of awakening spiritual values in the US, and gave support to the habit of prayer during the hard economical times of mid-19th century. Later on, in the 1960's, in different parts of the world, studies were conducted researching scientifically the reality of power of the prayer in healing.

In Science Daily of June 2009, Wendy Cadge, an expert on the intersection of religion and medicine in contemporary American Society, evaluated eighteen published studies of intercessory prayer conducted between 1965 and 2006. Prayers combined not only Christian prayers, but also those of other religious practices such as Buddhism, Judaism, and Islam. This opened a door to a scientific approach of the practice of prayer and the way it contributes, along with traditional treatments, to the comfort and help it might bring to patients.

Scientists continued to look with an analytical mind if there existed any proof of the power of prayer in healing. Many have heard or read about people recovering faster and better if prayers were made for them. It has also been established scientifically that people who pray regularly and who have strong spiritual beliefs have a better response to stress and a better immune system.

We can quote several scientific studies reporting results as "highly significant." In a study conducted in the San Francisco General Hospital between 1982 and 1983 in the Coronary Care Unit, the patients who received prayer as additional treatments, were healthier, needed less CPR interventions, less placements on the ventilators, less need for medications, and counted for fewer deaths. Dr. David Larson commented on a study made by Duke University medical center in Durham, NC, in 1998 proving that blood pressure can be lowered in response to prayer.

Virginia Commonwealth University in Richmond, VA, after studying 1,902 twins, published an article in December 1998 in "McCall's Magazine", which conveys interesting conclusions based on the difference of lifestyle in twins. Those having a rich spiritual life had better health and were less depressed. They had happier marriages, fewer had smoking and drinking habits, and enjoyed a more stable social life.

Dr. Koenig and Dr. Paragament, from Bowling Green State University in Ohio, studied the impact of the religion on health in 577 patients hospitalized for severe conditions. The ones with a strong faith, not only had better outcomes, but some also benefitted from a longer life. Even an atheist like Dan Barker, a spokesperson for the Freedom from Religion Foundation, was not surprised that this research indicates that religious thoughts can help in the healing process.

Furthermore, microorganisms such as bacteria, viruses, and fungi have been subjected to studies, under the assumption that these microorganisms cannot be influenced by positive or negative thinking, and cannot pray or influence themselves through autosuggestion. However, in the observations of prayer for bacteria done from faraway, Dr. Dossey in his book, "Be Careful What You Pray For," or Dr Jean Barry, in Bordeaux, France, on a study on Rhizoctonia Solani, a destructive fungus, found the results significantly positive. Dr. Daniel I. Benor, who evaluated these researches on healing bacteria through prayer, found that these results could be explained by chance only in less than one in a thousand.

"Therefore I say unto you, what things so ever ye desire, when ye pray, believe that ye receive, and ye shall have."

Mark 11:24.

Prayer is universally recognized as part of the customary way of life, and very few are the ones not believing in prayer and in its power.

Considering Prayer Therapy as part of Gentle Therapy, I have the intention to bring in another way of *looking at prayer – as a way to improve one's life and self-image.*

Prayer has transformed millions of lives; it helps to look deeper inside and reach higher up into the Universe. Prayer brings hope and opens doors of possibilities. We have heard many times of how important is the manner in which we pray; we all know that a prayer is granted with response if it is made sincerely, from the heart, and with the intention to do good. All this is true, and *a prayer should always be made in a respectful, honest, and reverential mode.* One must always remember: "Be careful what you pray for, you might get it."

"The one who comes from Heaven is above all. He testifies to what He has seen and heard. Whoever has accepted his testimony has certified this, that God is true... For He gives the Spirit without measure."

John 3-31

Gentle Therapy encourages the habit of prayer, making a link between the understanding of the psychological impact in our conscious and unconscious decisions and choices we make in life, and *the power we receive in changing our life when connecting with the divine.*

Gentle Therapy is intended to create a special state of mind, carried with us anytime and everywhere we want. It is not only about the instant we feel compelled to make an urgent and strong request at a moment of distress, - this is indeed also a time for a prayer, and it works as well, and one should not hesitate to make a prayer if he feels the need. However, it is important to *think of long term ideals, have a vision of your entire life and yourself, and to try to bring this vision to reality through prayer.* It is using the positive power of prayer to establish kind and elevated images of ourselves, construct the path of our existence, and define our character.

Regular practice of prayer helps to create a clearer mental picture of what we want in life, and what changes and improvements we ardently wish to see becoming reality.

For centuries people were influenced by cultural beliefs expressed in their respective religions, and grew immersed in the established norms of the moral standards of their time. This would further determine social and individual behavior and interactions. Thus, religious beliefs determine what was or is proper for that respective social group and institutes how to treat parents, spouse, and elderly, how to marry and how to bury the dead, and even what to eat and how to dress appropriately.

Now, let us just consider, based on each one's cultural upbringing, *what are our personal ideals*, and focus on them during our daily plea. Starting from the idea that there is no limit in what we can be or achieve, we must *envision in details the life* we pray for. Then being convinced that what we pray for will be granted, we focus all our energy and loving thoughts to that particular design.

No one should feel that his or her condition is less favorable or deserves less attention, for God listens to all prayers, from the most humble to the ones requesting a miracle.

For centuries we favored the idea that exceptional people, extraordinarily talented or intelligent, received some kind of transcendental genius, that they were born with and consumed by special gifts, during a very special mission during this lifetime. We accepted the idea that people with incomparable lives were just born exceptional, and we, common mortals, will have to agree to a more modest condition.

More modern psychological analysis of the character and destiny of exceptional people brings a better understanding to why and how they could achieve unusual exploits. Certain common traits came to surface, to define what is the difference between people of similar abilities to succeed or not. Surprisingly, it was not the IQ level, nor physical or material advantage that was the determining factor of one's success. What guarantees accomplishment in a subject is the vision of the intended goal, the finality of that purpose, becoming so important that it symbolizes a reason to live and die for.

We all have been inspired by someone, some real or fictional character, a relative, celebrity, or just a fleeting image, that made a strong impact in our life. In the way we look at the same socio-cultural aspects of the same generation, we can perceive the same thing in a very different way. Depending on our exposure to different life styles, cultures, and traditions we absorbed during our young life, we will be impressed by different images of what will become our ideals. These experiences will determine all the connections we made over the years, what we kept and consolidated on these mysterious pathways of our brain, that will find the reverberation with our soul, and this has nothing to do with anyone's intelligence capacities.

Steve Jobs, the inventor and founder of Apple products, when he was diagnosed with cancer declared: "Your time is limited, so don't waist it living someone else's life. Follow your intuition and your heart; somehow you will know what you truly want. Everything else is secondary."

Exceptional people, consciously or unconsciously, are determined, acquire a *high level of knowledge and self-discipline, and know how to control their actions and decisions with total concentration and determination*. They knew what they wanted to be, and had a larger vision of the world and humanity. These outstanding characters had in many instances high morals and deferential manners, a strong self-confidence, but above all, they wanted to mark their place and time, and through their lasting work, they will somewhat become immortal. Exceptional people knew that their task was beyond one self's existence, and they wanted to transcend the physical limitations of their own life. This way they were connecting with the divine.

It is true that *prayer is a matter of faith, and without belief there is no answer to prayer*.

"So we do not lose heart. Even tough our outer nature is wasting away, our inner nature is being renewed day by day. For this slight momentary affliction is preparing us for an eternal weight of glory beyond all measure, ... for what can be seen is temporary, but what cannot be seen is eternal."

Corinthians 4-16

The Gentle Therapy view of our spiritual life is to give importance to the *decisions we make and what we expect out of our actions, thoughts, words, and in particular our prayers.* Gentle Therapy supports the idea that reality will become what we think and what we believe. Gently *making order in different aspects and goals in life,* and inspired by people that motivate us to bring out our best, there is no limit on contemplating our future through prayer.

As said earlier, *prayer can be present with us at any time and any place*, as we don't have to be in a special place to talk to God. Our Creator made everything and is omnipresent; He listens and understands. Making a sudden demand when in distress, or saying a few words of thanks for unexpected blessings, should be always ready on our lips. But what we should consider in the long range is how we see ourselves in this lifetime, what we want to achieve and how we count for others. Because this life is important: it is not only precious, it is sacred.

This lifetime is a wonderful gift given to us to live it on this marvel that is our planet. Again and again we are in awe at the awesome sight of this unique place, its amazing beauty and richness. One can wonder why we are here and what is the purpose of our existence. We are in the quest of the meaning of our destiny, and during the time of prayer we try to penetrate this mystery, but also to shape our request following our desires and our principles.

Weaving the fabric of our prayers, *we must pay attention to its content*. As we continue to grow, our intention must be to dream of a life as wonderful and as fulfilled as the unlimited sky. This way, we want to create the image of this ideal person we want to be. From there we fashion our prayer with a clear picture of a sublime life under all aspects.

We can pray for a better health, profession, home, for friends, success, and the realization of our dreams. We can pray to find serenity and harmony, and be surrounded by beauty and love. Then, *believing with all our soul we release this image, and entrust God that He will make it our reality.*

God finds ways, wonderful and miraculous ways to answer to our prayers; He will do it for our best, and at the right time. We are probably not having the patience, and sometimes the faith to support our own demands, and then we realize how much better answer, after all, we got. So be thankful, and *be thankful for whatever comes into your life*; there are certainly trials and obstacles to learn from, but as difficult as they can be, *there is always a better time to come.*

And there is a promise to live by, here in this world as well as beyond: the promise is in John 14, when Jesus says: *"Do not let your hearts be troubled. Believe in God, believe also in me. In my Father's house there are many mansions. If it were not so, would I have told you that I go to prepare a place for you?"*

And God has many ways to bring us help and comfort; He sends us his messengers in many forms: an idea, a peace of music, an image, a sudden inspiration, and His Angels.

I believe in Angels, I believe in miracles. They happen all the time and at the right time. And they happen to everyone, no matter how aware that person might be. There are a multitude of testimonies of divine interventions, unexplained wonders that responded to frantic request of people in distress.

Have faith, *never lose the faith that miracles will happen*, that your prayers will be answered, and know that there are Angels on Earth. I also believe that there are Earth Angels; how many times have I witnessed the selfless kindness of someone that, with a particular gesture or word, touched my life and forever made a difference.

Everyone can become an Earth Angel and inspire others to expect happiness and goodness, and in their turn do the same. *You will recognize* when the opportunity will present itself; it is *your moment inspired by God*, to raise yourself, to enter and be part of His circle of love, to give and care for others, and feel the happiness that this will bring to you.

You can *start your day with prayers* for what is the most dear to you, but don't forget to *pray for others.* We all should be mindful of people in need all over the world, and make specific requests for the ones suffering from natural disasters, or going through hard times in their lives. When praying for people in need, or all of God's creatures and natural foundations, ask God to guide you on your path. He will send you the Angels, and create the circumstances for you to carry on the goodwill.

God said to him: "Because you have not asked for yourself long life and riches, but you have asked for your understanding to discern what is right, . . . Indeed I give you a wise and discerning mind; I give you also what you have not asked, both riches and honor all your life; no other king shall compare to you. And I will lengthen your life."

Solomon's prayer for wisdom. Kings 3, 5-14

We all should make the habit of having a *loving gesture for someone else every day.* Spreading hope, love and goodness will bring anyone the greatest happiness.

I would like to close this chapter with a prayer made by Rena Arnett, who, along with her husband, Toy, are pastors of the Faith Assembly Christian Church in Destin, Florida. This assembly, or "The Rock and Roll Church", is an example of the sense of community and friendship one finds here in Destin. Toy and Rena's prayers and warm inspiration gave me many times the encouragement I was looking for. Rena's prayer, One Day At A Time, says it all – just take one day at a time.

Rena's Prayer

ONE DAY AT A TIME

Precious Heavenly father,

The Bible says You live in the praises of your people. Psalms 150:6 "Let every thing that has breath praise the Lord."

Forgive us our sins as we forgive others. Lead us in the path You would have us to go.

All our yesterdays are gone, time took them away, and tomorrow may not be.

Today, the first thing, I will find quiet time in prayer, because prayer changes things.

Today, I will reclaim the peace for my life and reflect it towards others.

Today, I will have the courage for the great sorrows in life, and patience for the small ones.

Tonight, I will go to sleep in peace for God is awake.

Marinella F. Monk, MD

🚲

Place to visit: **_Destin, Florida_**

I visited quite a few places that life, in its mysterious ways, brought me to, and in many places I felt the close presence of God. I also learned with time, that His presence was everywhere and anywhere we happen to be. I understood nevertheless, that some places have for each of us very special meanings, and that we have been brought to them for special reasons.

So, I came to Destin, Florida, and moved here, in this other example of heaven on earth for me and for many others. I fell in love with this place at first site, when my husband took me here about 12 years ago, and showed me the area where he spent his summer vacation with his family. For Robert, it represented the reward after a school year, a well anticipated recompense of happy times to play in the azure waters, and fish on the pier at the dawn of the day, blessed moments of childhood with no worries and no schedule. An idyllic place to keep forever in one's heart and to restore the soul, just remembering the treasured moments spent here, a perfect example of memories any child should hold from family vacations.

The feeling of this place, situated on the northwest, or the Panhandle, of Florida, with its turquoise waters and sugar white beaches from Pensacola to Panama City, gave me the same thrilling happiness of leaving behind stress and frenetic life pace. And at that time I surely was under pressure and nervous tension, ready for a change. I was longing for a life that had for me a new meaning and orientation, and a place where I could have some personal time to enjoy it.

It was a hard decision to step away from a very rewarding medical practice at Houston Rehabilitation Institute in Houston, Texas, where I was medical director, leaving patients and friends I loved; but I realized that, with all my good intentions to slow down the pace at work, only by moving away could I better control my life.

And I will never regret this decision, since Destin was the answer to my prayers, the destined call where I could harmonize my medical practice and other interests in life. So we moved to Destin in mid 2002, after the dramatic wake up call of September 2011 reminding us how quickly life can change. Although I am still very busy, my life goes more smoothly from the office to my family, flowers, music, community activities, and even finding some time to write this book.

I feel so blessed to belong to a small but elite medical community, where medical professionals are driven to provide excellent care to patients, and assist each other in a friendly manner. Robert and I are privileged to meet many interesting people coming from all over the world attracted by this place where the nature, rhythm of life, and the friendly attitude of people brings to existence a quality rarely found somewhere else. It is refreshing to see, even when I am driving to work, surfers biking on their way to the beach holding their boards, and visitors leisurely wandering along and smiling happy and relaxed.

I know, what for a long time the inhabitants already knew, that Destin is a unique place, destined to attract people from everywhere, because of its natural beauty, but also because of the spirituality that it radiates.

Destin is located on the Emerald Coast, and extends over Okaloosa and South Walton counties, containing a string of beaches like Crystal Beach, Miramar Beach, and Santa Rosa Beach. Its geography shows that Destin is a peninsula stretching between the Gulf of Mexico and Choctawhatchee Bay. Once occupied by the Creek Indians who discovered the rich waters of the Gulf and the Bay, Destin offers clement temperatures in winter and summer. The four seasons create weather conditions that permit a variety of plants found on the mainland as well as in the tropics to grow. The natives discovered also that this enchanted place had a spiritual quality, with areas emanating a calming energy very much like the vortexes in Sedona.

Around 1850 Captain Leonard Destin from Connecticut, settled in Destin and a fishing camp was born. Nowadays, Destin is known as "The Luckiest Fishing Village in the World," and is situated at about equal distance of 50 miles from Pensacola on the west, and Panama City at its east. Near by are other communities like Fort Walton Beach, Seaside, Grayton Beach, Rosemary Beach, and Navarre.

Marinella F. Monk, MD

Destin, known mainly as a touristic destination, has a local population of roughly 15,000, but many of the 4.5 millions tourists visiting the Emerald Coast will stop to visit Destin. They enjoy the whitest beaches in the world, made of finely ground quartz crystals, the impossibly turquoise waters, state recreational parks and natural wildlife refuges, national seashores, and the October Fishing Rodeo and Seafood Festivals. Outlet malls and great restaurants are some of the many Destin's attractions.

People enjoy coming to Destin, not only for vacation, but many expressed that the veritable pull comes from the more mystical attraction they feel, the sense of filling a spiritual need, a soul hunger to replenish with energy the emptiness left by the city living. Visitors come to Destin to experience the value of immersing in total relaxation and beauty, to regenerate and find peace, and to restore the connection with powers above and beyond ourselves.

A very unique fact I encountered only in Destin, is that there is a strong spiritual community; once a year for instance, all the churches gather and consecrate one week of blessings, including the fishing fleet, marketplace, schools, real estate and tourism, family and individuals. Last year an imminent catastrophe menaced our beaches from the BP oil spill which occurred in April 2010. On the very date of June 3d less than one mile from Destin Pass, a large dark blanket of oil was approaching to our immaculate beaches. Well, there is no doubt in people's mind that a grace was granted to our community, after our pastors and people came and made ardent prayers of protection. It was indeed an act of God to spare the incoming devastation by diverting the currents and pushing away the oil. A commemorative plaque was engraved to remind all of us that that day we were given the proof of answered prayers of protection from the worst oil spill known in modern history.

I also feel that my prayers are answered to the life I longed of, finding professional satisfaction, peace, love, and beauty in everything I see around. And I count my blessings every day.

♫

Music chosen is **Messiah's "Hallelujah" by George Frederic Handel.**

Handel was born in 1685, when his father was 63 years old, and made future plans for his son to become a lawyer. However, the very young Handel had a strong inclination for music, and against his father's interdiction, found a clavichord in the attic of the house, where he played every time he could. He practically taught himself at an early age how to play the organ and the harpsichord. The story goes that when George Frederic was seven or eight years old traveling to Weissenfels to visit family members, Duke Johann Adolf I heard him playing the church organ. Impressed by the child's exceptional talent, the Duke asked Handel's father to allow the child to take lessons of composition and continue his organ study.

Handel's career did not go straight to music, since in 1702 he had to start studying the law at the University of Halle, but he also played the organ at the local Protestant cathedral, and in 1703 assumed the position of violinist and harpsichordist in the orchestra of Hamburg Opera. Here is where Handel started his opera compositions, writing *Almira, Nero, Daphne,* and *Florindo*, produced between 1705 and 1708.

Later in life Handel composed an enormous amount of beautiful baroque music: 42 Operas, 29 Oratorios, 120 Cantatas, concertos for many instruments, including 16 for organ, and Grand Concertos for orchestra. Handel liked to introduce unusual instruments in some of his works: viola da gamba and viola d'amore, small high cornets, theorbo, bell chimes, positive organ, and lyrichord.

Messiah was performed in 1742, and Handel arranged its performances to benefit the Foundling Hospital in London. Since 1750, *Messiah* was performed during two annual concerts throughout Handel's entire life, and *Hallelujah* as part of the Oratorio, describes the life of Christ. It was a commissioned work, coming very timely since Handel, age 56, was discouraged and covered with debts, and this commission changed the financial course of his life.

Handel set to work in August 1741, and during the 24 days he composed *Messiah* he never left his house in Brook Street in London. He rarely ate anything, and a servant after three weeks bringing food and worrying about Handel's condition, finally saw the composer open the door. Handel declared with tears welling down his face, "I think I did see Heaven before me, and the great God Himself."

Handel lived as a profoundly spiritual person, and his masterpiece made an extraordinary impact to the audiences. The King of England attended the premiere performance, and at the first notes of the triumphant *Hallelujah*, the king stood up, the audience followed, and from that time on, he established the tradition that *Hallelujah* will be heard standing.

After the first concert, Handel gave 400 pounds to free 142 men from debtor's prison. Later the proceeds of *Messiah* concerts benefitted to "feed the hungry, clothe the naked, and foster the orphan, more than any other single musical production." A person wrote:" Perhaps the works of no other composer have so largely contributed to relief of human suffering." Handel, although a Lutheran, accepted and helped people of all religions.

George Frederic Handel was afflicted with many trials in his life, from financial disasters to health problems, and he always reacted with good sense of humor and confidence in God. He suffered from several strokes, and had begun loosing his sight in 1750, when he wrote in a chorus "How dark, O Lord, are thy decrees. All hid from mortal sight." Handel became totally blind in 1752, but he continued to perform and remained involved in his works until his death on 14 April 1759.

Handel directed more than thirty performances of *Messiah*, and when Lord Kinnoul congratulated him for the "excellent entertainment," Handel replied: "My Lord, I should be sorry that I only entertained them. I wish to make them Better."

Beethoven considered Handel as "the master of us all, the greatest composer that ever lived. I would uncover my head and kneel before his tomb," he said. When it comes to other composers to learn from Handel's simplicity, Beethoven encourages them to "go to him to learn how to achieve great effects, by such simple means."

There was a review on Messiah stating that Handel "has done more to convince thousands that there is a God about us than all the theological works ever written."

CONCLUSION

Thank you for reading my book, and I hope that you found inspiration and help from it. This book is the product of scientific research and spiritual inquiry, with the intention to harmonize those two aspects of our existence, as we live it everyday.

During the journey my reader was taken through the various chapters of this book, I tried to share my own feelings and memories, making the experience more personal. In this book I poured my heart and my soul, hoping that sharing the difficulties I encountered in my life, may help others find solutions and answers to theirs.

If you think that reading this book was helpful for you, please let me know, and share it with someone else. Thank you.

ACKNOWLEDGEMENTS

Since my childhood I grew in admiration for people able to enrich humanity with their knowledge, wisdom, or the artwork they left behind.

Learning more from the accomplishments of some exceptional people from my readings and visiting some places marked by extraordinary events, or cultural treasures, helped me to accumulate an extensive amount of information.

Throughout this book I tried to share my impressions and my enthusiasm generated by scientific discoveries, unique places of natural or human design, and spiritual feelings. The blending of these elements together resulted in my personal opinion expressed in this book.

When writing various chapters of this book I found inspiration from many sources, from readings, music or other forms of art, and from places I visited. I named the source of information or quoted texts every time I could remember, with my best intention to acknowledge the exact origin of the information provided.

I do not intend to appropriate the authenticity of any research or literary work. Any error of interpretation is mine only.

In my life I have been blessed to know many incomparable people who with their outstanding personality or generosity have forever marked the trajectory of my life. My parents, music professors, teachers, and mentors such as Dr. Agnes Moon, will always have my deep gratitude and admiration.

My love and recognition goes to my family and friends. My patients, as many became friends and family, are dear to me for their trust in me, and the inspiration I found as we were building our relationships.

As always, my loving thoughts and special recognition go to my husband Robert, my companion, and my best friend. I am grateful for the assistance, trust, and encouragements he happily offered. For the joy, for the soul searching and excitement while growing together during the mysterious paths of our lives, and for all the happiness, I am grateful.

COMMENTS FROM READERS

In our present day, with diminishing of civility, I find your book most important in the effort to restore it. Would that we all give heed to the gentleness you advocate in your book, for daily living, four ourselves, for others, the planet. Our society would indeed be most civil!

Thank you for writing such a fine and important book. I hope that you will have many readers that enjoyed it as much as I did and see its importance for lour day.

Reverend Anthony Fasline, Retired Priest
Diocese of Youngstown, Ohio

~~~

Dr Monk shares her healthy concepts about life in Gentle Therapy. She gives a special voice to approaching life while protecting yourself from the world stresses that are buzzing for your attention. She uses a comprehensive guide including travel visualizations, and classical music suggestions to help you embrace her concepts, moving you along to a happier lifestyle.

Beverly Bryant, author of "The Adventures of Nani Choe Choe" and "Goddess of the Ring"

~~~

Gentle Therapy is a life-giving template for anyone, especially those who are feeling conquered by depression or illness, or simply tired of living a "vanilla" life. Marinella Monk has the experience, vision, spirituality, and gentleness of articulation that causes the reader to expand one's vision enormously. It will help those desiring travel to zero in on destination goals, complete with suggested itinerary. It will guide those who have a desire to relate to music, to have a "playlist" upon which to draw from. I believe it will expand one's perceived potentiality toward life in general. I have just passed it on to my husband as my comments as I was reading, persuaded a desire in him to also read this book. I believe it will benefit us as a couple as well. I will read this book again, and will have my play list recorded so that I may listen to *the corresponding musical suggestions as I read each chapter. A wonderful addition to anyone's library.*

Andrea Soltis, Destin, Florida

~~~

As Marinella Monk writes: "Gentle Therapy is to see and connect with the divine anywhere and anytime. It is letting the Light of Creation pour into your soul and fill you with healing energy . . ." Dr. Monk, both an artist and scientist, is a lover of beauty. She finds it in music, paintings, architecture, science, and people and nature everywhere. In her extensive travels, she has found the thread that connects us all and can heal us, if we, like her, can recognize it and appreciate it in everything and everyone. I hope you enjoy her book as much as I did.

Francois-Marie Bénard, Actor, Poet ("The Dream Of Life")

~~~

As we left the parking lot yesterday, I was truly inspired by the first few paragraphs in your book in regards to facing problems. Surprisingly, it was like God had sent words of inspiration that jumped off the page that I happened upon. Last night I read the first two chapters. I felt as though we should all live our lives much more in tune with your very words. This morning, for the first time ever, I awoke at 6:00 am and lay in bed with the TV off and the blinds open, overlooking the sound, in utter silence. The peace my family has always enjoyed and I was raised in, but quickly forgot. Cell phones ringing, email arriving, places to be, people needing me here and there, responsibilities all pull me away from the very roots and reason my family has long remained in this area. Looking out the window at the tranquility of the water as the sun started to lighten the sky, I then started to listen to Beethoven Piano Concerto No5 "The Emperor". I found myself with times of utter peace followed by times of excitement and upward lift as the music played. Today has been a wonderful day. Thank you for sharing.

Charles Kuebler, Emergency Room Physician's Assistant